Praise for

PREDICTABLE PROFITS

"In a shifting world, Stu McLaren champions the transformative power of memberships, leading the way in community building and business growth. Stu empowers entrepreneurs to share their expertise, create impact, and establish sustainable, worry-free business models. Highly recommended!"

— **Gabby Bernstein**, #1 *New York Times* best-selling author of *The Universe Has Your Back*

"I've watched Stu empower countless entrepreneurs to build sustainable, high-impact businesses. In *Predictable Profits*, he reveals the blueprint for transforming one-off sales into a reliable stream of recurring revenue. It provides everything you need to launch a successful membership site."

— **Michael Hyatt**, *New York Times* best-selling author of *Platform* and publisher of the *Full Focus Planner*

"Stu McLaren's work has had a massive impact, helping us grow from a tiny little one-person business in a 500-square-foot apartment to a seven-time Inc. 5000 Fastest-Growing Company. *Predictable Profits* is an absolute must-read book for any entrepreneur seeking to bring predictability to their income and life in a highly unpredictable world."

— **Ryan Levesque**, #1 national best-selling author of *Ask* and *Choose*

"Stu is a special human. His depth of knowledge when it comes to building a membership-based business is second to none. Even better is his depth of caring and obsession to see others succeed . . . that's a lethal combination in the best way possible."

— **Dean Graziosi**, multiple *New York Times* best-selling author and co-founder of Mastermind.com

"Creating my own community online has been deeply rewarding at many levels. If you've got an inkling to do the same, Stu is *both* the OG and the cutting edge in this space. This is the book you've been looking for."

— **Michael Bungay Stanier**, author of *The Coaching Habit*

"If you want to build a successful membership, then devour this book! It is going to teach you everything you need to know to build a thriving membership and a recurring revenue stream."

— **Carrie Green**, author of *She Means Business* and founder of the Female Entrepreneur Association

"Not only is this a game-changing guide for any entrepreneur looking to build a recurring revenue stream, this book will help any entrepreneur radically improve their method, messaging, and marketing. This book isn't just a membership primer, it's a business builder."

— **Bari Baumgardner**, founder of SAGE Event Management

"Stu McLaren is the real deal. Working alongside him at Membership.io, I've seen firsthand the depth of his expertise in the membership space. His insights are practical, powerful, and actionable. Stu is a leader you want in your corner if you're serious about growth."

— **Dan Martell**, *Wall Street Journal* best-selling author of *Buy Back Your Time*

"Stu McLaren is a genius when it comes to memberships. He knows how to make you believe in your business and convince you to take action, and he'll show you how to build something that lasts. If fear is holding you back, Stu's your guy to help you push through."

— **Jennifer Allwood**, business coach for Christian women and author of *Fear Is Not the Boss of You*

"Stu McLaren shows entrepreneurs how to create businesses that are powerful, profitable, and purpose-driven. If you're ready to redefine wealth through connection and service, Stu's insights on memberships offer a transformative path forward."

— **Patrice Washington**, founder of the Institute for Redefining Wealth

"What we've learned from Stu McLaren has been life-changing. Thanks to his teachings, we built our membership site the right way from the start, resulting in a thriving community of thousands and a stable, recurring revenue stream."

— **Scott Paley**, co-founder of the Nonprofit Leadership Lab

"Building a membership business is one of the simplest ways to create consistent, reliable income—and Stu McLaren is the undisputed expert to help you succeed. He combines a proven approach to financial growth with a deep commitment to integrity, values, and lifestyle."

— **Susie Moore**, author of *Let It Be Easy*

"Memberships are the magical bridge from month-to-month anxiety to sustainable year-over-year growth, and Stu is exactly who you need to shepherd you across that bridge. For decades Stu's been the go-to guy for memberships, and now he's packed all that wisdom into one easy-to-use book."

— **Shelley Brander**, founder of Knit Stars

"Following Stu McLaren's practical and simple strategies, I launched my first membership and added multiple six-figures in annual recurring revenue to my bottom line. Thanks to Stu, I'm no longer stuck in perpetual 'launch' mode. He has made me fall in love with my business all over again."

— **Alex Cattoni**, founder of Copy Posse

"After reading *Predictable Profits* and integrating Stu's teachings on recurring revenue and memberships into your business, your life and your business will never be the same. I have been recommending Stu to all Hay House authors for more than a decade now, and I can say all have been blown away by how their businesses change for the better when they apply his easy-to-integrate teachings."

— **Reid Tracy**, CEO of Hay House

"This book lays out the ultimate blueprint for building a successful membership model in any industry, in any niche. Stu genuinely cares about helping others succeed, and I can't recommend him enough."

— **Sarah Williams**, author of *One Box at a Time*

"Recurring revenue is essential to scaling a sustainable creator business. Stu is the master of scaling memberships to millions in recurring revenue."

— **Nathan Barry**, founder of Kit.com

"I was about to close down my struggling membership when a friend suggested I connect with Stu McLaren. In clear, actionable steps, Stu teaches exactly how to structure a membership in a way that delivers high value without creating overwhelm. "

— **Susan Bradley**, founder of The Social Sales Girls

"If there's anyone who truly understands what it takes to build a stable, thriving business, it's my dear friend and mentor, Stu McLaren. He really cares about people, and his words have the power to reshape your business into a steady, profitable venture—and a business that brings you joy and provides the impact that you want to make."

— **Suzi Dafnis**, CEO of HerBusiness

"In today's fast-paced market, Stu makes an undeniable case for the power of recurring revenue as the foundation of stability and growth. His approach isn't just about generating income; it's about building a loyal, engaged community that turns customers into lifelong advocates."

— **Peter Johnston (PJ)**, founder of Persephone Investments

"Stu McLaren is known in my world as the membership guy—and for good reason. I've used his teachings to create both low-end and high-end memberships that provide me with recurring revenue all year long. Whether you're just starting or looking to scale, this book will give you the road map to make it happen."

— **Sigrun Gudjonsdottir**, online business consultant and international speaker

PREDICTABLE PROFITS

TRANSFORM YOUR BUSINESS FROM ONE-OFF SALES TO RECURRING REVENUE WITH MEMBERSHIPS AND SUBSCRIPTIONS

STU MCLAREN

BUSINESS

HAY HOUSE INDIA
New Delhi • London • Sydney
Carlsbad, California • New York City

Hay House Publishers (India) Pvt Ltd
Muskaan Complex, Plot No. 3, B-2, Vasant Kunj, New Delhi – 110070, India

Hay House LLC, P.O. Box 5100, Carlsbad, CA 92018-5100, USA
Hay House UK Ltd, 1st Floor, Crawford Corner, 91-93 Baker Street, London W1U 6QQ, UK
Hay House Australia Publishing Pty Ltd, 18/36 Ralph St., Alexandria NSW 2015, Australia

Email: contact@hayhouse.co.in
Website: www.hayhouse.co.in

Cover design: Narcis Rus • *Interior design:* Nick C. Welch
Interior photos/illustrations: Delia Hrimiuc

First published by Hay House India, 2025
10 9 8 7 6 5 4 3 2 1

ISBN 978-93-6611-879-6

Printed at Thomson Press

MIX
Paper | Supporting responsible forestry
FSC
www.fsc.org
FSC® C010615

Hay House is committed to a sustainable future for our business, our readers and our planet. This book is made from Forest Stewardship Council® certified paper.

To my kids, Marla and Sam: Be curious, follow your interests, and always give with a generous heart.

To my wife, Amy: Thank you for always believing in me and expanding my world of possibility. I love you so much.

To my parents: You gave me two of the greatest gifts—the confidence to be me and the courage to go for my dreams. Thank you.

To our community: Together we are changing our own little corner of the world. Thank you for inspiring me to keep sharing this material.

CONTENTS

FOREWORD

by Amy Porterfield

You know that feeling when you meet someone, and everything just clicks? It's like meeting your best friend for the first time—the kind of connection where you think, *This is it. This is my person.* That's how I felt when I first connected with Stu McLaren, my "work husband" and the peanut butter to my chocolate.

From the moment we met at a mastermind to standing on stage with his amazing wife (who, coincidentally, is also named Amy) raising over a hundred thousand dollars for their charity, I knew Stu's values, drive, and passion were perfectly aligned with mine.

And I realize that starting a foreword for a business book called *Predictable Profits* by talking about best friends might seem a bit unconventional, but this is Stu's book—and it's the only one I'd introduce this way.

That's because Stu's value goes far beyond business strategies; it's about who he is at his core. He inspires everyone around him, leading with heart and letting his passion for helping others shine through in everything he does. This foreword is unlike any other I would write because Stu himself is unlike anyone else.

As you dive into these pages, you'll quickly understand why. His captivating personality and enormous heart, coupled with his infectious energy, make his vision for building wildly profitable businesses truly inspiring.

Stu is all about crafting a meaningful, lasting impact in business that aligns with his deeply held core values.

I witnessed this firsthand during a recent Q&A session Stu led for my community, made up of thousands of online digital course creators. What began as a conversation about building memberships and their perfect complement to digital courses soon evolved into something far deeper.

In his usual heartfelt way, Stu shared how precious these years with his kids are and how quickly time is passing as they grow up right before his eyes. He went on to say that this is his "why" and how it shapes his approach to creating predictable profits, running his business, and living his life.

His vulnerability moved everyone, including himself, to tears. It became clear that his membership model and philosophy around business isn't just effective; it's meaningful because it's rooted in purpose. It's about creating a life that allows you to be fully present for the things that matter most.

And it's that same sense of time passing quickly that Stu highlighted during the Q&A, which I want to leave you with as you prepare to dive into this book and create predictable profits in your own business.

Like Stu, I've learned that building a successful business isn't about having all the answers from the start, it's about taking fast action and not wasting any more time, even when things feel uncertain.

The sooner you take that first step, the sooner you can learn, grow, and refine your approach. Waiting for the "perfect moment" only delays your progress, while taking action—however imperfect—sets everything in motion. And the truth is, there's never a perfect moment; there's only the moment you decide to begin.

You don't need to have every step perfectly mapped out. In fact, many successful entrepreneurs began with just a "starter idea" and refined their business along the way. Take my own journey as an example: I started in client work, transitioned to teaching about

Facebook ads, and now focus on educating others about creating digital courses. This evolution was driven by adapting and refining my business model, proving that where you start doesn't have to dictate where you end up.

But I wouldn't have reached this point—where I love the work I do and enjoy more financial and time freedom than I ever imagined possible while working my 9-to-5—if I hadn't taken that first step before I felt truly ready.

What's key is focusing on progress, not perfection. I cannot stress this enough: your business growth and profits will happen when you start before you're ready and consistently show up, test, learn, and refine.

You don't have to constantly produce groundbreaking work, but if you show up consistently and deliver value, your audience and customers will know they can rely on you. This trust and reliability are the true foundations of predictable profits.

It's this continuous action that leads to lasting success, and that's exactly what Stu embodies in his business approach. And while you're taking action and implementing what Stu teaches in this book, remember that you don't need to have all the experience in the world.

One of the most empowering lessons I've learned is the importance of focusing on your 10% Edge. You don't have to be an expert at everything or have decades of experience to offer value. All you need is to be a few steps ahead (about 10%) of your audience. Your unique perspective, combined with the ability to guide others from where they are to where they want to be, is what truly sets you apart.

Lean into what you know, share your journey authentically, and trust that your audience will resonate with your message. This mindset will help you build a business that connects with people, changes lives, and reflects your core values—just as Stu has done with his own.

As you turn these pages and absorb the wisdom Stu shares, keep in mind that the journey to predictable profits requires dedication to your business and a commitment to a life that honors your deepest values. Each chapter will guide you toward financial success and help you build a legacy that resonates with who you are.

While Stu provides a blueprint for creating wealth and enriching our lives, it's your responsibility to put these principles into action. By doing so, you're investing in your future and the future of those your business will impact.

Ready yourself for a journey that will transform how you think about work, success, and the mark you want to leave on the world.

INTRODUCTION

The Life-Changing Power of Memberships

Hello, I'm Stu! Stuey to my friends, "babe" to my wife, and "Dad" to my two kids. Here's why I'm qualified to talk about the magic of memberships. Back in 2005, I was just a young 20-something guy who grew up with a dream of building my own business. The only problem was, I was still living in my parents' basement. I wish I could tell you that I had the perfect plan and knew exactly what I wanted to do. But here's the reality: I was clueless. I didn't know what kind of business I wanted to create, what products I was going to sell, or even the first step in trying to figure it all out. I was only clear about one thing: I didn't want to be wearing a suit or tie, and I definitely didn't want to be stuck behind a cubicle.

In my quest for clarity, I was pouring all my energy into my own personal growth. I was attending seminars and reading every self-help book I could get my hands on, trying to figure out how to make a great living. This was also when "digital entrepreneurship" was just becoming a thing, and I was fascinated by the idea of building a viable business using the Internet, all from my teeny, tiny town of Waterford, Ontario, Canada (population 4,000).

I was lucky enough to find a mentor who asked if I would be his "affiliate manager." Essentially, I would be training people how to effectively sell his products. In his words, he said that I was "good with people," had a solid marketing mind, and kept things really simple—which made me perfect for this position.

It turned out, this role became a catalyst for the rest of my career. As an affiliate manager, I was behind the scenes on all the major marketing campaigns. I also had the opportunity to meet many of my mentor's friends who were helping promote his programs. Things were rolling, and we were getting incredible results. Very soon the word spread, and I found myself with many other digital creators in my inbox asking me to help manage their affiliate programs. Within months, I had a bona fide business with multiple clients that paid incredibly well. I was living the dream (and still living in my parents' basement!).

After a couple of years of consistent growth, my girlfriend, Amy, and I got married and purchased our first home. Everything was rocking. Until it wasn't. Every time we had conversations about having kids, I could feel my stomach turn. I wanted kids. In fact, becoming a dad was one of the things I looked forward to the most. But I soon realized that my business model wasn't going to work if I wanted to be a present husband and father. I was up early and working late. I was burned out and overworked from launching multiple times a month and managing people. This business I had created was supporting us in all the ways that I'd dreamed . . . except I had no life outside of work because my schedule was at the mercy of my clients. That's when I realized that if I continued running it the way I was, my relationships with the people that mattered most (my wife and future kids) would suffer. Something had to change.

One day during this period, Armand Morin, a client and friend, said, "Why don't you start a membership site?"

"What's that?" I asked.

"It's a site where people pay monthly to learn from you, and you teach them how they can manage their own affiliates and launches."

Huh, I thought. *I could get regular, predictable monthly income just from teaching what I already know how to do. And there are no limits on the number of people I could serve. And I'd get my schedule back and be able to start generating recurring revenue. That sounds pretty great.* It was the perfect shift from working with clients one-on-one to then being able to serve hundreds (even thousands) at a time. So I got to work creating my first membership site.

I went through a few iterations of this. My first idea was to launch a membership teaching others how to grow and manage their own affiliate program. But I struggled with the tech, and it was preventing me from doing the thing I was hoping to do—teach! So, at the encouragement of my friend and colleague Tracy, we decided to create our own software. He took the lead on the development, and I focused on the vision of making it easy to use for people like me. In less than a year, we were powering tens of thousands of membership sites. Being behind the scenes of these sites, I quickly learned what was working and what wasn't. While many memberships plateaued, there was a small group that consistently grew year over year. That's who I paid attention to. I noticed that these successful entrepreneurs did a few key things differently. Eventually I launched a membership about memberships, sharing these best practices. (Meta, right? Told you I was the membership guy.)

Fast forward a few more years, and I launched the first version of The Membership Experience™ course, where I walk people through the whole process of conceptualizing a membership idea—to creating the content strategy, the marketing plan, retention plan, and so much more. My goal was to hit $500,000 in revenue to validate that this could be a viable business. Instead, before we closed out the first day of the launch, we hit $1 million. By the end of the launch, three days later, we were at $3.35 million. And thousands of people had begun their journey to starting their own membership businesses.

Today, I run an eight-figure business teaching people how to start memberships. I've refined and relaunched the course multiple times, consulted with first-timers with zero audience and no business experience all the way to *New York Times* best-selling authors, as well as nine-figure business owners. The goal is always the same: to help them create a more stable and predictable revenue stream in their business. And the best news for you is that I've coached tens of thousands of people through the process you're about to learn in every market you can think of. That brings me to this book.

THE MAGIC OF MEMBERSHIPS

What if I told you that instead of hoping to find new customers every few weeks for your business, you could know with certainty *exactly* how much revenue you were going to make month after month? You wouldn't have to worry about where your next sale will come from, or how you are going to pay the bills. No more starting each month at zero; no more hoping someone stumbles upon your website or through your door.

How would that change your life? Maybe you could focus on other things, like delivering a great service or doing the work you actually like doing instead of constantly stressing about finding new customers. Or maybe you could spend more time with your family and just have a little extra brain space to not stress so much about next month's revenue.

Well, my friend, it's possible. These kinds of predictable profits in your business are not a fantasy. For thousands of people in my community, they're the life-changing reality they're living right now. All because they started a membership business.

To define our terms here, by "membership" I mean a business where customers pay a monthly fee for access to your goods or services, instead of a one-time transaction model. You've probably often heard of these described as "subscriptions." Tomato, tomahtoe. In my world, we call them memberships because we're interested in creating communities, not in treating people like a number.

Membership sites are magical. Unlike a traditional business that is dependent on one-time transactions, a membership business not only creates predictable recurring revenue every month, but that revenue compounds—meaning, the more you put into it, the bigger it grows each month. In a traditional business, you hit the sales "reset button" every single month and you're left wondering how many sales you'll make. With memberships, you never start from zero. You start every month with the momentum that you gained the previous month, which is compounded on the previous month before that!

As far as business models go, memberships are king. In fact, in the last 10 years, the subscription economy has grown by 435 percent![1] Everyone from solopreneurs to Fortune 500 companies is realizing the enormous benefits of having a monthly recurring revenue model.

Memberships are all around us. Don't believe me? Take a quick inventory of all the memberships you subscribe to. Go ahead, I'll wait. I'm willing to bet the list looks something like this:

1. Netflix, Hulu, Disney+, etc. Come on, you know you subscribe to at least one of these entertainment services. Ninety-eight percent of consumers do, and 75 percent subscribe to two or more.[2] And yup, they're memberships.
2. Amazon Prime. About 65 percent of Americans who shop on Amazon are Prime members,[3] so there's a good chance you are (or someone you know is!).
3. Peloton or a gym.
4. Software. From Microsoft's Office suite to web-hosting services, it's likely some part of your computer or business needs or runs on a membership model.
5. Food delivery services. From Uber Eats to Instacart to Home Chef, most of these have a monthly recurring model.

All kinds of businesses are transitioning to the membership model because of the predictability it creates in revenue. Take Mary-Claire Fredette, for example. She has a massage business and was tired of wondering how much money she'd make every month just hoping customers would rebook with her. She implemented a super-secret tactic you'll learn about in Chapter 16 and launched a membership. Right out of the gate, she had 16 people join her membership for $75 a month, which guaranteed them one massage a month. Now, Mary-Claire knows exactly how much money she'll make each month, *and* her clients are getting a more regular service at a great rate.

Years later I caught up with her, and my heart sank when she said she hadn't done another launch since that first one. "I haven't launched again because over the last three years, I've maintained 80 percent of my membership customers and I haven't had to!" she exclaimed quickly.

If you've ever considered starting a membership business, now is the time. Let me tell you why. First of all, **memberships create certainty**. This is a completely different way to do business because it creates stability. Knowing how much revenue is coming in each month eliminates stress and puts you in a place to make better decisions. And when you're not stressed about money, you run your business with far more confidence. You hire better, invest better, market better, and ultimately lead a better life.

> ***Knowing how much revenue is coming in each month eliminates stress and puts you in a place to make better decisions.***

So much of the stress for entrepreneurs comes from the ups and downs of sales. When a promotion hits and sales are great, we, as entrepreneurs, feel great. But when a promotion doesn't land, or a client ends the contract, or even worse, the economy crashes or a pandemic hits, stress skyrockets. This kind of stress inevitably impacts every other area of our lives—down to our marriages, families, friendships, and health. But when we have stable, recurring revenue, we are far more insulated from these outside factors.

Now all of that "feels good," but what does having recurring revenue actually do for the bottom line? This is the second benefit of this kind of model: **it just makes good money**. When you look at the state of the economy and tech at large right now, you can see the majority of bigger companies are moving toward recurring revenue from subscriptions—companies like Apple, Amazon, Google, Spotify, and the *New York Times*. Even Peloton makes more money from its subscription workout programs than the actual sales of the bike. Panera and Burger King have monthly coffee clubs you can belong to with a monthly membership fee. And that's something I want you to notice. Businesses all around us are moving to a recurring revenue model, because that's how you create stability.

The best part (and perhaps what I'm most passionate about) is that this kind of recurring revenue **allows people to be more generous with their money**. This is the third main benefit. Giving is a deeply held value of my family and my company. And I tend to attract big-hearted, generous entrepreneurs who have good intentions and want to give as well. But that's hard when you can't predict your revenue. Memberships and subscriptions don't just change the financial future of your family, they can literally change the world by allowing you to give to causes you care about on a recurring basis. A sincere hope of mine is that when you're consistently making more, you'll also have the confidence to be able to consistently give more. As our membership sites grow, so can our giving, and so can the impact we're able to make in the world.

Here's what I know for sure: if you have a membership as part of your business—whether it's your entire model or used in conjunction with other offers—your life will change. Let me prove it to you with a little thing I like to call Membership Math. Let's say you started a membership today and charged people $25 a month. You probably have thousands of Facebook friends—don't you think you could find a measly 20 who could benefit from your goods or services? And if you found just 20 people to join your membership, you'd make $500 a month. What could you do with an extra $500 a month?

Okay, let's take this up a notch and say you found 40 members. Now you're looking at an extra $1,000 a month. Amazing, right? You probably have more than 40 people's numbers stored in your cell phone. That's totally doable. Now I know not everyone in your phone is interested in your membership. I'm just saying this to demonstrate how a few people can bring a big boost to your bottom line, and that you almost certainly already have access to them somewhere in your sphere of influence. And if you already have an audience of thousands . . . phew, think about what a difference it would make in your business with thousands of members paying predictably every month!

If you find 80, then you're looking at $2,000 per month. And this all assumes you're only charging $25 per month. Most people in our community run memberships that cost more than that. If you charged $50 per month at 80 members, then you're looking at $4,000 per month. All with fewer than 100 customers! What could be possible for you and your family if you had an extra $4,000 that came in month after month? Could you scale back some at work? Travel more? Go on more dates with your spouse? Spend more time with your kids? Finally do that home renovation? Fund meaningful projects? It's all possible with a membership business.

> ***You are just a few decisions away from a whole new life.***

My company has served more than 17,000 people in every kind of market you could possibly imagine—from photography and calligraphy to fitness, finance, music, art, health, dog training, therapy, yoga, acting, homeschooling, belly dancing, and balloon animal making. The thing that makes me the proudest is seeing people go from zero business experience, potentially never even imagining themselves owning a business, to creating meaningful recurring revenue for themselves and their families every month.

My friend, you are just a few decisions away from a whole new life, if you want it. Memberships have changed everything for me and the tens of thousands of clients I've worked with. You're going to hear example after example of business owners just like you who have moved from one-time transactions to recurring sales. I promise to teach you everything I know if you promise to give it your best effort. I'm rooting for you and can't wait to dive in. Deal? Deal. All right, let's get started.

HOW TO GET THE MOST OUT OF THIS BOOK

Before we get to the good stuff, here are a few tips to help you get the most out of this book.

1. You do not have to implement *all* the ideas here. You have permission to take what you need and/or what interests you most right now. This is supposed to be fun and helpful, not stressful or overwhelming. Just taking action on a few things can make a monumental difference in your business.
2. Go in with this mindset: "How can I make this work for me?" There are plenty of different kinds of memberships, just like there are plenty of different kinds of people. Not everything will resonate or feel applicable to you. But I promise there is something you can learn in *every* chapter if you just constantly ask yourself, *How can I make this work for me?*
3. These chapters are bite-sized for a reason. One of the things you'll discover is the value of helping your customers gain quick wins. If you finish a chapter or two at a time, you'll experience exactly that! It will dramatically help you build momentum.
4. The audiobook has extra stories, interviews, and tidbits that you won't find here, so I encourage you to get that as well for the full experience.
5. There are *tons* of external resources that you can find at predictableprofitsbook.com. Anything you can think of to help you build a membership site, it's there. This website will also include any tech or templates used in this book and will be updated as needed. Most importantly, in-depth case studies of dozens of our students are there to inspire you and show you exactly how to implement every concept in this book.

Scan this QR code to immediately access these resources as you read along.

PART I

THE FOUNDATION

The foundation of having a membership business is all about making the shift from the old way of doing business to the new way. One-time payments, stress-filled months, and missing important moments in life are out. Recurring revenue, restful sleep, and having fun are in. But first, you have to lay the foundation that sets you up for long-term success without burning yourself out.

In Part I we're covering everything that makes the rest of this process work. First, you'll do a little exercise to determine if a membership model is right for your particular business or idea. Then I'll teach you how to do plenty of market research (the easy way!) and get crystal clear on who you serve and how. We'll refer to all of this information often throughout the book, so pay attention, stay open, and get excited. It's time to try something new!

CHAPTER 1

MAXIMIZE PROFITS, MINIMIZE STRESS: MY MEMBERSHIP PHILOSOPHY

Everything in this book is built on the back of this philosophy: minimize stress, maximize profitability, and do less.

1. **Minimize stress.** Running your business should feel light and simple, but multiple surveys of small business owners[4] reveal that "financial concerns" are the number-one source of all stress for small business owners. Meaning, when we're experiencing cash flow issues or inconsistent sales, stress skyrockets. The good news is there are strategies that we can use to avoid all of these stressors.
2. **Maximize profitability.** Though I'm all about fun, this is a business. You and I are in it to help a whole lot of people, but we're also in it to make money. And we can help a whole lot more people when we make a whole lot more money. The way we do that is by keeping people happy. If people are happy, then they're staying. And if they stay, you maximize the profitability of your membership. It is *far* more

profitable to keep an existing member than it is to find a new member. That essentially means that you and I are in the business of making and keeping people happy. It's simple and easy. And it's precisely how we maximize profitability.

3. **Do less.** People often go down a lot of little rabbit holes chasing shiny objects, but at the end of the day, it's much more efficient to focus on the few things that are going to make the difference—the 20 percent that will produce 80 percent of the results. At the end of the day, there are many things you can do to improve and grow your membership, but very few of them will actually move the needle. Do more of what works, less of what doesn't. In the pages that follow, I'll show you what those are. If you focus on them, you'll make a lot more progress.

That's it. Don't you want a life with little stress, plenty of money, and without your business consuming every hour of the day? I know I do. So with that, roll up those sleeves, and get yourself ready to create a membership that is right for your business.

LESS OF WHAT
DOESN'T
DO MORE
OF WHAT
WORKS

CHAPTER 2

WILL THIS WORK FOR YOU?

By far, the most common question I get in my line of work is: Will a membership work for my business, idea, or market? And here's what I always do: I walk people through a very simple series of questions to find out. Let's do it together right now. There are only three questions I want you to consider, and if you can answer yes to any one of them, that's a big, bright, flashing green light for you to move forward with your membership. Here they are:

1. Is there an ongoing problem my market is looking to solve? For example, if your market is health and wellness, there are tons of problems in that niche that people are constantly trying to solve, like losing weight, gaining more energy, or feeling better. Maybe you're a therapist or coach and your clients are desperately seeking help repairing their relationships. If there is any recurring problem that your potential customers are staying up late Googling, that's a sign that you've hit on a great membership idea. To do a little research, head to your search engine of choice and type in some keywords that have to do with your idea or market. Let's take the dog training market as an example. Pick one keyword, like "dog training," and add in a place on the Internet where people might be talking about that topic. Like "dog training

forum" or "dog training Facebook group." If you find a whole bunch of groups, videos, forums, websites, etc. where people are engaged in asking questions, you can probably find tons of potential problems your customers have.

2. Is my market looking to learn a new skill? This pertains to all the creative niches where your customers might be looking to master something like learning how to paint, play an instrument, cook, grow a business, or even parent better. Most people in the world are interested in learning something new. If your market has a skill they'd like to build, thumbs up for you. That's a potential membership. Here's a quick exercise: head back to your keywords again. If you find several different formats of information, that's a good sign—especially if there are tons of downloads, reviews, and comments. That means that plenty of people are consuming this information. Are there signs that people want to learn and develop skills around your topic? Are there lots of books on it? Courses? Those are all indicators that people are not only consuming lots of information about your topic, but that they want to get good at it. Jackpot.
3. Is my market looking to simplify something in their life? Who in the world doesn't want their life to be easier in some way? I've had lots of students come through my course who can answer yes to this question. They have memberships that provide lesson plans, weekly recipes and shopping lists, or templates for social media, ads, or newsletters. All of these ideas simplify a task that many people find time-consuming. They're often tasks that have to be done regularly. Lots of successful memberships help people get hours of their week back by streamlining something for them.

Did you answer yes to any or all of the three questions? If you did, this is your signal to go for it full steam ahead. Memberships will work for just about every market. With your idea now affirmed and some speedy research under your belt, you can confidently move forward. Now let's take a look at a few reasons why someone would join a membership to help you serve customers even better.

CHAPTER 3

THE 6 REASONS SOMEONE JOINS A MEMBERSHIP

Before you can build a membership site and decide what to offer your customers, you need to know why someone would join one in the first place. That makes sense, right? In my experience, there are six core reasons people join a membership. Many people join for more than one, though most of the time, there is one *main* reason. I call this the primary reason. The other benefits you offer would be secondary reasons. Let's run through them.

1. NEED

The most common reason that people join memberships: **Customers have a true, genuine need for what it is that you are providing, month after month.** Let me give you a couple of examples to frame this. Patty Palmer is an art teacher who provides lesson plans to other art teachers. If you have ever been or known a teacher, then you know that lesson planning inevitably spills over into the evenings and weekends. It can drain your energy and prevent you from being truly present in the classroom. Patty's lesson plans enable teachers to get more creative with the actual lessons, all while freeing up their evenings and weekends. This membership fulfills a need and keeps teachers purchasing and joining regularly to have pre-prepared lessons sent to them each and every month.

Software companies follow a similar model where customers pay on a monthly basis. These are companies like Slack, ClickFunnels, Kit, or our own membership platform Membership.io. They provide tools that our team uses every single day, and I don't know how we would operate without them. This ongoing need is what makes them powerful (and why people stay).

2. MASTERY

When a customer wants to learn how to get better at something, we call it mastery. Often, we see memberships like this in markets such as photography or calligraphy, where it takes time to learn the skills of using a camera or developing beautiful penmanship. That's where a membership comes into play.

My students Levi and Tony are membership business partners who teach people how to play guitar. You can't just watch a few videos online and become the next Eric Clapton. People need real instruction to learn this skill beyond the fundamentals, and they continue to stay in the membership because they have an interest and passion for fully mastering the guitar and developing their craft.

Heidi Easley teaches people how to grow a thriving paint party business—everything from the setup to planning to finding customers. (Note: this is a wake-up call if you've ever found yourself worried that your idea is "too niche." Take some inspiration from Heidi. There's room for just about everything out there.) Her customers continue to stay because she helps them grow their revenue and improve their party-planning skills month after month.

If you're teaching somebody something, it is *very* rare for them to learn what to do or how to do it and then instantly master it. Your membership gives them that space to get better and better at not only understanding what you're teaching but to truly develop those skills in a profound and meaningful way.

3. COMMUNITY

You'll see "community" pop up a lot in our discussion, as it is a *huge* reason people join most memberships. **Customers want to be surrounded by others who are on a similar journey.** We see this show up in a variety of formats, including masterminds, associations, and clubs. It can be hard to feel like you're the only one of your friends or family who is interested in something. These community-based memberships bring people together as they learn something new or explore a topic.

Jewish wedding expert Karen Cinnamon runs a membership that helps Jewish brides plan their weddings. She provides cheat sheets and checklists to help them with planning, but the real value of the membership is in the community she's created. Jewish brides join to connect with others in the same shoes and receive endless support and advice. They even stay subscribed long after they're married because of the relationships they build!

One of the *amazing* things about the Internet is that you can have the most unusual interests and it's virtually guaranteed that someone in the world is just as passionate about it as you are. Instead of feeling alone, we can make people feel supported and inspired. That's why community is important—and it's a big reason why people will join a membership.

4. ENTERTAINMENT

People join memberships for entertainment. Yup, that's right, plenty of **customers join memberships just to have fun**. Let me ask you this: Do you have a Netflix or Spotify account? Disney+ or Hulu? Maybe you have a zoo membership where you can go an unlimited number of times per month. Or a boat membership where you can make use of a boat as much as you'd like.

If you have any of these memberships, you're not looking to learn a skill or find community. And you certainly don't *need* the membership. You're just looking to be entertained, to enjoy something. Plenty of businesses thrive by providing these kinds of services. But instead of hoping that their customers come back, they've set it up so that they know with certainty they'll return. If you're offering something that brings people joy, don't underestimate what people are willing to pay for it and how often they'd like to consume it.

For example, recently my wife and I went to try a float tank at a local spa. It's like a giant bathtub full of salt water, and when you lie in it, you float because of all the salt in the water. It can be very relaxing. After we finished and were paying, the receptionist asked if we would like to join their membership. "Tell me more," I said.

Essentially, instead of paying each time we visit, we could get access to the spa as often as we liked for a monthly fee (which was cheaper than a couple of sessions). More access for less. Simple, right? The customers get what they want (unlimited access) and the business gets what they want (predictable revenue). It's a win for both sides. But in the case of the spa, there isn't a need they're meeting and we're not mastering anything. And we're not really building community while lying there in silence. However, it's a valuable form of relaxation and entertainment.

Entertainers like comedians, singers, and songwriters can also create thriving membership businesses from their crafts. Customers value having intimate access to entertainment and content from creators that they can enjoy as often as they'd like.

5. WANT

The next reason that somebody would join a membership is that they have a want. This is as simple as it sounds: **customers just want something**. For example, Nancy Case has a membership called Taffy2You, where she sends out monthly boxes of saltwater taffy to subscribing customers. And guess what, they *love* it! It's absolutely delicious. (I've eaten many bags of Nancy's taffy!)

Another student of mine named Oscar started a membership that is all about growing beehives. You might be wondering, *Why would somebody join a membership about beehives?* If so, that's totally fine. You're likely just not in Oscar's ideal audience. But those who *are* his ideal customers understand that bees are important to our environment. What Oscar is doing is giving people a chance to be a part of something that helps the Earth. People with the desire to have a positive impact on the environment are drawn to this business. There's also a secondary community aspect to Oscar's membership, where beekeeping enthusiasts can connect with others with this same passion, as it may be challenging to find them in their "real" life.

6. CONVENIENCE

Sometimes **customers want a task to be easy and more convenient.** Years ago, when my daughter was born, my wife and I realized that we could no longer continue eating crappy food because now we were responsible for another little human being. We needed more energy and to just feel better overall. We had to figure out how to create fresh, healthy meals, something we'd never worried about before.

Here was the problem: neither Amy nor I enjoyed cooking. We love to eat, but we hate to cook. That's when I went online and did a little search. My initial search was for "fast, easy, and healthy meals," and one of the first results that popped up was a membership site called The Fresh 20. The promise of the site was clear: "Fresh, healthy meals in 20 minutes or less." Yum, yum, give me some! It took me less than two seconds to sign up because they made things easy by providing recipes and shopping lists, and walking us through how to prepare the meals—all of which saved us time and energy.

The fun part was, years later I got to know Melissa Lanz, the founder of The Fresh 20. I learned this entire multimillion-dollar membership began from her kitchen table. She could see people were overwhelmed with the millions of free recipes online and all the conflicting information about this diet and that diet. At the end of the day, people just wanted the convenience of somebody doing the thinking for them. And that's what has made her membership a huge success.

There are plenty of other kinds of memberships that fall into this category as well. Memberships that just make people's lives better and easier by saving them time. One of our clients, Andrew Krauksts, has a membership where he provides Facebook ad templates for real estate agents in Australia. His customers don't have to go learn all about Facebook, how to run ads, or copywriting. And, they don't have to spend time obsessing about what copy they're going to use to sell their homes. It makes being a great real estate agent much easier and more convenient because Andrew is serving them ads that get results in their local area. Plus, this is the part of the job many agents hate. At several hundred dollars a month, Andrew's membership is on the expensive side, but it makes sense for a real estate agent because even if it only helps them sell one more home throughout the entire year, the whole membership pays for itself, and then some.

To see Andrew's full case study, head to predictableprofitsbook.com.

To recap, the reasons people will join your membership will vary, but they generally fall into one of six categories: need, mastery, community, entertainment, want, or convenience. When you're crafting your membership, get clear on the primary reason that somebody will join. There may be multiple reasons, but when you get clear on your *primary* reason, it is going to help you focus on what to highlight in your marketing and your content.

CHAPTER 4

HOW TO DISCOVER WHAT YOUR CUSTOMER IS REALLY THINKING

Here's the deal: the better you know your customers, the better the experience you can create for them. Plus, it becomes *so* much easier to attract them to your membership because they'll feel seen, heard, and understood on a level they've never experienced before. That's why it's important to take some time to get to know the people that you serve on an intimate level. If you can get familiar with the problems and challenges of your ideal customer, you'll be able to provide the solution that will attract them to your membership.

I'm going to give you a variety of prompts to help you get to know your ideal customers. This is going to shape the way you speak to and serve your audience. The best way to do this is to address the different types of problems that your market faces.

I first learned about this from the great, multiple *New York Times* best-selling author and entrepreneur Donald Miller. In his book, *Building a StoryBrand*, he talks about two different types of problems: external and internal. External problems are the most common type and usually come to mind first. My "simple Stu" definition of the external challenge is whatever someone would type into Google when they're looking for a solution. For example, if somebody has a dog that pees all over the house, that's an external problem (speaking from experience here). They type, *"How do I stop my dog from peeing in the house?"* and want to go from a dog that pees all over the house to a dog that is perfectly potty-trained. Or another common one is, *"How do I help my toddler sleep well at night?"* In a dream world, you want to go from a child who's up all night to a child who sleeps restfully—ideally, as quickly as possible.

Now here's the thing I want you to realize: when it comes to serving and selling, most business owners make the mistake of stopping at the external problems.

But not us! We are going to examine the even-more-important second type of problem: internal. This is the conversation that's really going on in your customer's mind. It has more to do with their fears, doubts, and anxieties. These are the things that often remain unspoken but weigh heavily on people's minds.

With my first software company, on paper, everything looked amazing. It was a phenomenal company, I had a great business partner, we had a great team, and we were serving over 70,000 online communities and memberships. But eventually, there was a part of me that realized I was ready for another chapter in my career. The problem was, I didn't know what that next move would be.

I was scared to move forward. And I wasn't really talking about it to anybody because I didn't have any clarity yet. In my mind, if I was going to make a big move, I should probably know what the next "thing" was going to be. What would I even say? "I know everything is great, but I want to quit"? Then one night, I was on a camping trip with my wife and daughter. We were staying in a cabin. It was the middle of the night, pouring rain. My wife was sleeping soundly beside me, but all I could hear was the raindrops coming down, landing loudly on the tin roof. As I lay there in the pitch-black, I had a moment of clarity. I realized it was the time to sell WishList Member.

A few minutes later, Amy woke up and said, "Are you okay?"

"No," I said. "I think I just made a big decision. I'm going to sell WishList."

"Okay, tell me why," she replied.

"I just feel like I need to create space for my next thing," I said. I know, not the most reassuring answer, right? I almost felt silly saying it, wondering if Amy would think that I had lost my mind, especially because we had a young family. But she didn't. She patiently listened and asked a few clarifying questions. Then I remember her saying, "Okay. I'll support you. We'll figure it out."

It's a good story now, but in the moment of telling her, I wondered, *Will I be able to repeat my success? Was WishList a one-hit wonder? Will people still want to do business with me now that I'm no longer associated with WishList?* These thoughts, fears, and feelings were my internal problems and challenges.

When you can address what's going on in your audience's minds and hearts in those same kinds of what-keeps-them-up-all-night moments, people feel understood on a deep level. And when you give voice to their internal problems, that's when you can really connect with them. They get that, *wow, they're reading my mind* type of feeling. And sometimes it's so subconscious they don't even realize why they're drawn to you in the first place. You seem to understand them better than they understand themselves. So where do you even begin if you want to dig deep like this?

First, start with the external problems, since those usually come the easiest. I want you to jot down at least 10 problems that someone interested in your topic might have. And don't overthink it; just come up with a list of as many external problems you can think of that they might be Googling—big problems and small problems alike.

Let's take "parents of a newborn" as an example. Some problems they might have include:

1. Baby is not sleeping
2. Parents' lack of sleep
3. Teething
4. Cutting fingernails
5. Breastfeeding challenges

6. I can't stop worrying if my baby is breathing
7. Constantly calling the doctor
8. Traveling with babies
9. Reaching developmental milestones
10. Loss of intimacy with partner

If you have kids, you've probably experienced many of these issues. If you need some more inspiration, you can also read comments under books on your topic on Amazon or Reddit threads. See what people are regularly asking about or what they liked and disliked about the information they have. Do you notice any patterns? Any recurring questions?

Next, head over to the ole Googler. Or your search engine of choice. Type in an external problem and combine it with a place on the Internet where a discussion about that topic might be happening, like we did in Chapter 2 when you did some preliminary research. These could be Facebook groups, threads, forums, product reviews, YouTube videos, blogs, etc. When I type in "baby is not sleeping forum," the fourth result is a post on a forum titled "Desperate. Four-month-old won't sleep day or night." In the post, a mother goes on to use key phrases like "feeling desperate," "battle," "hopeless," "last resort," "nothing is working," "read all the tips," "exhausted," "mood is low," and "breaking point."

1. USE THESE WORDS TO IDENTIFY INTERNAL PROBLEMS.

Helping people with their internal problems is the real way you're going to serve them. You might be helping parents get their baby to sleep, but the true value in what you offer is in relieving the stress and shame in those early newborn days. What you're reading in these forums, groups, and comment sections is essentially *why* people want to solve the external problems. What deeper challenges arise because of their external problems? Reading into the data I found about parents of newborns, I could infer that this woman feels shame, fear, hopelessness, desperation, and frustration. She's afraid this will never end. She wonders if she's a good mom or if she's doing something wrong. These are the internal problems you want to note about your ideal customers.

2. THE LANGUAGE THAT YOU FIND IN YOUR RESEARCH IS THE EXACT WORDING YOU WANT TO USE WHEN YOU BEGIN MARKETING YOUR MEMBERSHIP.

Your people will be drawn to you and feel like you're reading their minds because you're using words they've actually used! This isn't a magic trick—they've just already given you the exact way they would describe their problems, in their own words. So take note of these words and phrases because you're going to use them again soon. And when you do, your audience will immediately feel a deep connection. Between us, having this deep understanding of my market has been one of the secrets to my success. And it will be yours now too! So take your time on this. Go ahead and do this research on your customers. Get into their minds and figure out how they speak.

CHAPTER 5

THIS SIMPLE TOOL MAKES ATTRACTING YOUR AUDIENCE EASY AND EFFORTLESS

Now that you've done some deep research into the problems your customer is facing, and how they would describe them, it's time to create your Messaging Map™. This is a device that you will find invaluable in your sales copy, messaging, and overall communication with your audience. It is a simple yet powerful tool that you will use repeatedly in your communication about your membership. It clearly shows the journey of where your customers currently are to where they want to go, as well as the transformation your membership offers. Whether you are engaging with your audience, mapping out your sales messaging, or creating content for your membership, it will be your go-to resource. Here's how it works.

Take out a sheet of paper and draw a line across the page, followed by a straight line down the middle. You could probably do this on the computer somehow, but I'm an old-school guy and prefer paper or a whiteboard. This will create two columns. Label the left-hand side "Now." This column represents the current state of your market—what they are thinking, feeling, and doing right now *before* they are part of your membership. Then label the right-hand side as "Future."

This column will explore what your market aspires to think, feel, and do in the future, *after* they join and learn from you.

Once you have the two columns, brainstorm single words or short phrases that describe what your market is thinking, feeling, or doing. And the reason we want to use single words or short phrases is that when you create contrast between their "now" world and their "future" world, it becomes *very* easy for your market to understand the transformation that's possible. We're not just offering a bunch of stuff. People aren't buying videos or PDFs or anything like that. Not *really*. They're joining your membership because they want some kind of outcome. At the end of the day, the most important offering inside our memberships is a transformation. And this is where the Messaging Map becomes a powerful tool.

Let's use an example from the quilting market. Imagine a woman in her 40s to 60s who is new to quilting and look at where she is *now*. She may feel **hesitant** because she has never tried it before. She might also feel **overwhelmed** because of the abundance of videos, strategies, and tactics she found when she did an initial Google search of how to start quilting. She is probably **confused** about where to start. She may **question her ability to learn** quilting, **doubt her creativity**, and **hesitate** to take the first step. These are the thoughts and emotions she is experiencing in the current moment.

In terms of her actions, she may be **thinking** about quilting but likely **not actually doing it**. She might be **consuming a lot of free videos** online without making any progress because of her doubt and overwhelm. She's not experiencing any tangible results. And worse, she probably has a **stack of materials** that she bought with good intentions of quilting, but she just hasn't gotten there. Plus, as that stack of fabrics and materials grows, so does the **frustration of others** she may be living with. Perhaps her husband or kids have made a few comments. And my guess is, this woman is **starting to feel guilty** because she has spent money, purchased all the things, but still hasn't done anything yet.

Can you feel the detail in describing this? Can you see how we're beginning to paint a picture? The more descriptive you can be here, the better. Refer to your research and get a good list of your customers' struggles in the present day. That's the market's current state.

Next, shift your focus to the future. What are your customers going to think, feel, and experience after they join your membership? If you find yourself stuck coming up with ideas, here's a tip: think of the opposite of what is in the "Now" column. For example, instead of being hesitant, she will be **confident**. Instead of being overwhelmed, she will **feel clear**. And rather than questioning her ability, she is **excited** to quilt because she knows that she can do it. Her actions will transform from thinking about quilting to **actually quilting**, trying new techniques, and **completing projects**. And the best part is that her loved ones are gushing about her, telling everyone about her projects. Extended family is even asking if she would **create quilts for them**!

> ***You're not just selling a service; you're offering a transformation.***

Can you feel the difference between these two worlds? All we are doing in this Messaging Map is contrasting the "old world" vs. the "future world." Just the other day I saw an ad targeted to parents for children's building blocks that said, "Imagine sitting down and drinking your entire cup of hot coffee in the morning because your children are so entertained." *That's* what those parents really want—to have a little peace in the morning to drink their coffee because their children aren't bothering them.

Do you see what you're doing here? You're not just selling a service; you're offering a transformation they're looking for. **When you create this contrast for your audience, it becomes obvious to them that your membership is the fast path between where they are and where they want to be.**

Here are some examples of what this looks like for different niches. Remember, what works for other markets can often work for yours too, as the feelings of fear, anxiety, overwhelm, and confusion are universal when starting something new.

Membership for Empty Nesters

This membership is designed for parents whose children have all left the home. It helps them get back on track, find purpose, and live life to the fullest.

Now (without membership):

- Running out of time
- Too old to pursue dreams
- Torn between family and career
- Wanting change
- No time to change
- Overwhelmed

Future (with membership):

- Excited to make the most of their time
- Never a better time
- Perfect balance
- Clarity and direction
- Lots of time
- Peaceful

Aspiring Writers Membership

This membership helps aspiring writers go from feeling stuck and uninspired to writing consistently and excited about their work.

Now (without membership):

- Insecure
- Feel stuck
- Lonely
- Self-critical
- Afraid of being judged
- Confused about where to start
- Inconsistent

Future (with membership):

- Confident
- Lots of momentum
- A loving community of like-minded people
- Permission to explore
- Supported
- Clarity and direction
- Writing regularly

All right, next up, I'm going to teach you exactly what to do with all of these descriptive words and the two worlds you've outlined.

YOUR
MEMBERSHIP
BECOMES
THE
BRIDGE
BETWEEN
TWO
WORLDS

CHAPTER 6

HOW TO DESCRIBE WHAT YOU DO SO THEY GET IT AND WANT IT

Have you ever experienced one of those awkward moments when someone asks, "What do you do?" and you really don't know what to say? I've felt this a ton of times in my life. Imagine the looks on people's faces when I try to tell them that I teach others how to create memberships—blank stares. If you're not a doctor or a lawyer or a one-word, easily understood profession, this can be hard. I've been doing the same thing for over 15 years, and my parents still can't describe my occupation. And this is especially true if you're an entrepreneur. Why? Because we inevitably do a lot of different things. You're "multipassionate," as my friend and ultra-entrepreneur Marie Forleo would say.

But here's the thing: if you want to have a membership, you have to be able to talk about it. That makes sense, right? You have to be able to clearly communicate what you do. I assure you, you can overcome those awkward moments. Not just so you can feel better at cocktail parties, but more importantly, so you can attract the right people for your membership.

I have good news for you—the work you did with your Messaging Map in Chapter 5 will come into play here. And real quick, did you take a moment to create your Messaging Map? (If not, I get you, but please go back and do it.) Because now we're going to turn your Messaging Map into a *positioning statement.* A positioning statement is a clear and succinct description of your membership and target audience. It explains how you fill a market need.

Let's continue with our example of the quilting market. In our Messaging Map, we discussed what the quilters are thinking, feeling, and doing now, as well as what they will think, feel, and do in the future after experiencing the transformation provided by your membership. Here's a simple framework to then transform the information into a simple positioning statement using three words from the "Now" column and three words from the "Future" column:

"I help ________________________________ go from
[market]

____,
["Now" word/phrase #1]

____, and
["Now" word/phrase #2]

____ to
["Now" word/phrase #3]

____,
["Future" word/phrase #1]

____, and
["Future" word/phrase #2]

____."
["Future" word/phrase #3]

By selecting keywords from your Messaging Map, you can create a powerful positioning statement. For example, for the quilting market, it might look like this:

> I help new quilters go from overwhelmed, confused, and not creating any quilts to confident, excited, and producing gorgeous quilts that others are raving about.

This method is straightforward. We take words from the first list and plug them into the formula, and then we take words from the future list and plug them in too. It may take some time to identify the most compelling problems or challenges your market faces, as well as the transformation they're looking for. But once you have it, the formula makes it easy to communicate how you help your market. The contrast between the two worlds creates magic, and the transformation will be irresistible to your audience.

Let's explore a few more examples. Think about the music lessons market, specifically where someone wants to learn how to play the guitar. We might say: "I help brand-new guitar players go from not knowing any notes, chords, or songs to playing songs with ease, jamming with friends, and being a guitar hero around the next campfire." We're highlighting the journey from where they are to where they want to be.

Or back to our parents-of-newborns example. You could say: "I help parents of newborns go from having a baby who is not sleeping, has you up all night, and feeling utterly exhausted during the day to having a baby that sleeps on a schedule, peacefully through the night, with everyone waking up refreshed." The contrast between exhaustion and restful sleep is definitely going to resonate.

Here's one more for the artists. An example positioning statement could be: "I help new artists who are scared, intimidated, and apprehensive about showing anyone their work transform into talented, confident artists who are proud to show and sell their art." See how this allows you to connect with your audience and clearly communicate the value you provide?

Before we move on, I want to address something else—the perfectionist in you. It's important to remember that this positioning statement will evolve over time. You may discover stronger words or phrases that will resonate more with your audience. You might even be able to simplify the statement down to one powerful word instead of three. But the key is to start mapping it out today. As with every action in this membership-building process, you can always refine and improve it later. The important thing is to get started and let people know what you do and how you help them.

Take some time to revisit your Messaging Map. Plug in a few words from the "Now" column and a few words from the "Future" column to create your positioning statement. Keep it tight and concise. Focus on the words that best describe what your market is experiencing now and the ones that best describe the future they wish to have. The more accurate you are, the more your market will feel seen, heard, and understood. Better yet, if you know anyone in your target audience, ask them! This exercise may take time, but it's worth it in the long run to get this as accurate and compelling as possible.

ACTION STEPS

1. Run through the list of questions in Chapter 2 and decide for yourself if a membership site will work for your business. (Spoiler alert: it will!)
2. Decide on the primary and secondary reasons someone would join your membership.
3. Research your market's hot-button issues.
4. Create your Messaging Map. Write out your "Now" and "Future" columns.
5. Fill in the blanks from page 30 and write your positioning statement so you can clearly communicate how you help people.

PART II

ATTRACT YOUR PEOPLE

Welcome to Part II! Now that you're clear on who you're going to help, it's time to get in front of the right audience. As Jason Fried and David Heinemeier Hansson say in one of my favorite books, *Rework*, "All companies have customers. Lucky companies have fans. But the most fortunate companies have audiences. An audience can be your secret weapon."

Here we'll break down the process of building your audience because, at the end of the day, you can have the greatest membership in the world, but if nobody knows about it, you're never going to be able to help anyone or build a viable membership business. This section is all about how to get in front of the people you can help. And don't worry, there's no fake, pushy, salesy, or smarmy methods here. Growing an audience is just about helping people.

No matter where you are in your membership journey, whether you are just starting out or already have an established company, growing your audience is fundamental to growing your business. In fact, you should *never* stop growing your audience. It's something that you'll continue to do, no matter how many members you have.

Audience-building mainly consists of two things: your e-mail list and social media platforms. They work together like this: the main goal of growing your audience on social platforms is to direct people to get on your e-mail list. You own your e-mail list. It's a business asset. Yes, it involves expanding your reach on different platforms like Facebook, Instagram, YouTube, TikTok, and more. However, the challenge with solely relying on growing an audience on these platforms is that they can disappear at any moment due to decisions made by the platform owners. They could change their algorithms or change in some way that might prohibit you from growing, maintaining, or contacting your audience. You'd lose your ability to generate sales. Think of these platforms as a rented house. You can stay there, but you don't own it. So you don't want to be solely dependent on them.

It's crucial to build your audience while simultaneously moving people from social media (or anywhere else) to your e-mail list. You own that list and can guarantee every time that your message with land in someone's inbox. The main way to expand your audience and grow that e-mail list is by creating content that helps people in some real way and effectively establishes your authority. The best part is, you don't need a massive audience of thousands or tens of thousands to begin building momentum for your membership site. Tracy Holmes had an e-mail list of only 87 people and barely any social media presence and welcomed 100 new members when she started her color membership! She helps creatives (or any color-lover) deepen their understanding and use of colors, educating them on hues, tints, shades, and tones. She created a physical color card collection and academy.

With the strategies that you're about to learn, you can quickly build your audience in a meaningful and impactful way. Just a few hundred people can make a significant difference in building momentum for your membership. And if you already have an established audience, these tips will amplify your existing efforts and help you find even more fans.

The work you put into growing a larger audience, especially one that is highly targeted, will pay dividends. This part is action-packed, so get ready and let's go!

CHAPTER 7

THE CIRCLE OF AWESOMENESS

The best way to experience long-term success in business is to help people get a result they're looking for. If you help people get what they want, you'll always be in demand. The main goal here is to solve people's pressing problems. And the good news is, you should already know what those are because we listed them out in Part I.

The entire aim of posting content on social media and YouTube, sending e-mails, speaking, blogging, etc. is to help people experience a win. Say it with me now: "Show up and serve people." These success stories don't have to be monumental. *Quick wins* is the name of the game. Because of your research in Part I, you are now intimately familiar with the challenges of your market. You have information that will help these people. Share it! That's all we're doing here. Don't overcomplicate this.

I want to introduce you to something called the Circle of Awesomeness™. It boils down to teaching your audience in your area of expertise, helping them achieve results, and then (with their permission) celebrating those achievements *publicly,* in as many places as you can. People who are experiencing the same problems are attracted to what you do because they want the same results as those you've already helped. When people see others succeeding, they become interested in what you offer and are more likely to join your e-mail list, community, and membership. Basically, they see the results of others and go, "Whoa, that looks good. Give me some of that!"

The process starts with posting something helpful or getting someone to opt in for your list builder. And then when your membership is up and running, this next step would be moving someone from being an e-mail lead to being a paying member. So the process looks like this:

Social Media → E-mail Subscriber → Paying Member

For this flow to work, the key ingredient is helping subscribers and members achieve quick wins and gain momentum. Once they experience any kind of win, you encourage them to share their success stories with you via e-mail and/or online somewhere, like on social media, making sure to tag you if possible.

The most valuable marketing asset that exists is a success story. It doesn't matter how small it is, you helped someone! In my business, the quickest win is usually helping people define the market they serve. But quick wins come in many shapes and sizes like welcoming their first member, seeing their members get results with what they're teaching, or improving their retention rates.

> ***The best way to get people to share their wins with you is to simply ask them.***

These stories show your audience what's possible for them if they continue learning from you. It's not just you saying, "I promise my thing is great!" Now you have others vouching for you. You have powerful social proof that your teachings work. And that creates **belief** that what you're teaching is possible, and it's possible for them! This inevitably leads to more people signing up . . . which leads to more people getting results. And that's why this is called the Circle of Awesomeness.

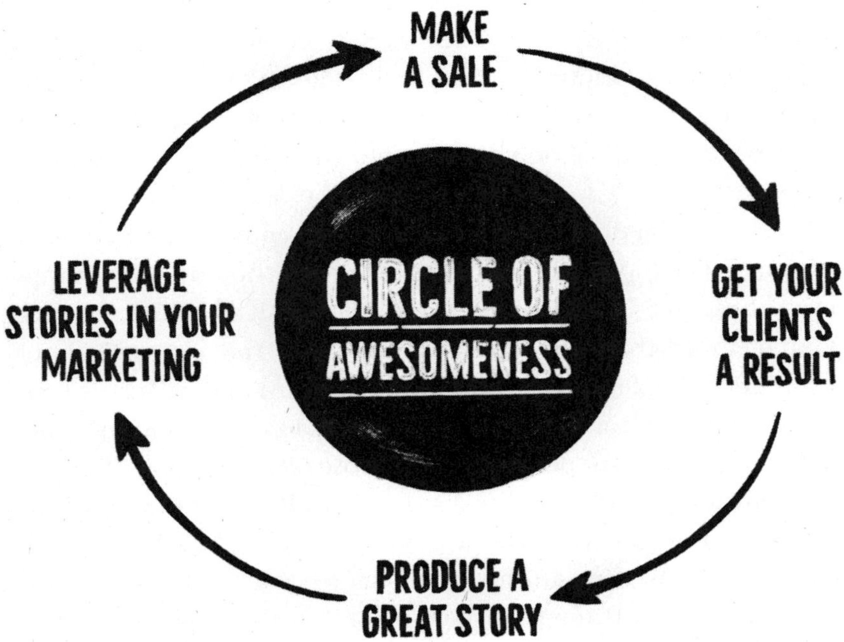

The best way to get people to share their wins with you is to simply ask them. Reach out via e-mail, comment in a Facebook group if you have one, or post the question on social media. "Hey! How's it going so far? I'd love to hear any wins you've experienced." Something as simple as that works.

I do this constantly with new members inside The Membership Experience, my flagship membership course. As soon as people get their very first member signed up, we encourage them to post in the community and then celebrate the heck out of them. In fact, I do this during the launch of The Membership Experience before people even officially join. I challenge them to do a founding member launch (more on this in Chapter 16) or put out feelers online for who might be interested in a membership around their topic. Every time, I have hundreds of people come back to the next training already experiencing progress because they took action on what I shared. They're psyched to see interest from their audience (no matter how big or small it currently is). Plus, it's powerful, encouraging, and motivating for everyone else. Their progress inspires more people to take action because they can see the results happening in real time.

All of this applies to both building your audience and growing your membership. Gushing about your people should be woven into everything you do. It's far more powerful to gush about the results of your members than it is to talk about yourself. If all I do is talk about my results, people will discount what I'm saying and will chalk it up to "Stu is special" or "it will work for him but not me." But the more you share about your people, the less those gremlins appear.

For example, let me share a story about Bonny Snowdon. Four years ago, Bonny didn't have an online business, but she did have a passion for drawing animals with colored pencils. So she started sharing—mainly through Instagram. She decided she could better support her audience to draw by establishing a membership. Two years later, her business crossed the million-dollar milestone, again, teaching people how to draw realistic animals with colored pencils!

Time-out. Do you see how powerful that is? Aren't you a little curious to at least take a look at Bonny's Instagram and membership site? You should, because they're awesome. My point is, stories are a super powerful way to showcase the value of what you offer and are very effective in building a strong community around your brand. Always, always, always be collecting more stories and expanding your library of successes from the people in your community.

> We have a full case study with Bonny at predictableprofitsbook.com, where you can learn more about her inspiring journey.

But while the Circle of Awesomeness is the most valuable marketing tool you have, it should also be a guiding principle as you build your membership. The whole purpose is to help people. To support them, teach them, encourage them, and move them closer to their desired outcome or result. Whatever the reason for your membership, your main goal is always to get someone a result. It's a win for your members, but it's also a win for you. And the better you are at getting your members results, the more profitable your membership will be.

Your own goal right now is to go out and get just *one* story by helping *one* person get *one* win. You *can* help people. You have something special to offer. I know putting yourself out there can be scary. But it's much, much easier if you have some evidence under your belt that proves your stuff works. Create that for yourself by helping people. It'll give you the encouragement and momentum to keep going.

> ***The better you are at getting your members results, the more profitable your membership will be.***

I'll end this chapter with the story of Joy Anderson, an amazing member of our community. For 10 years, Joy ran a preschool. It was going great and generating close to $30,000 per month in revenue. Although that may sound like a lot, Joy's family was over $400,000 in debt because of student loans. So with that burden, combined with all her monthly expenses, she was still struggling to get out of debt. She was run down, depressed, and burnt out. She wanted her life to slow down, but she was worried she'd never be able to stop working.

Eventually Joy decided to sell her business. This helped with the debt some, but Joy still needed a way to make money for her family. The next year she started a membership for preschool owners. She'd had such success with her own, maybe she could help others. That first year was a struggle, so after another year, she invested in The Membership Experience. In 10 months she multiplied the number of her members by 10 and has now generated over $3 million in revenue. And the best part is, the predictable revenue month after month from her membership allows her to take off as many months from working as she needs to. All because she started serving her audience and celebrating their success.

CHAPTER 8

WHAT DO YOU STAND FOR?

Jim Edwards, a marketing friend of mine, once said, "Love me or hate me, there's no money in the middle." Those words really stuck with me. What he meant was: you have to stand for something.

This goes beyond just having a mission and vision statement; it involves understanding your principles, the ones that will ultimately attract customers who resonate with your philosophy. To make a big impact—in your customer's lives, in the world, and yes, even in your bank account—getting clear on your values and beliefs is key. It shapes your membership and builds an intimate connection with your customers. For a long time, I wasn't entirely clear on this in my own business, even though I thought I was. But it wasn't until I heard someone say something so contrary to what I believed that I truly understood what my own values were.

I vividly remember watching a video from Gary Vaynerchuk on a Friday before Christmas. Now, let me be clear, I have great respect for Gary and his work. We even purchased hundreds of copies of his first book and did an interview with Gary (you can see it at predictableprofitsbook.com). However, when I was watching this particular video of Gary's, something didn't sit well with me. He emphasized the need to work long hours, grind, and hustle relentlessly to achieve success. He even mentioned how he was working late on a Friday night while everyone else had gone home to be with their families.

In that moment, it became clear to me that my values were different. I believe in the importance of spending quality time with my family, especially during the holiday season. I realized that I wanted to create a business that allowed me the freedom to be with those who mattered most. I actually didn't take pride in being at the office and "grinding" until the wee hours of the morning. That's *not* why I got into business. I wanted to be home with the people who mattered most to me, and I could feel myself getting worked up at the thought that hustling was the only way to experience success. This realization led me to create a video expressing my beliefs and values, highlighting the importance of building a business that serves our lives and gives us more time with our loved ones.

The response to that video was incredible. People resonated with my message and expressed their support. And, by the way, there were plenty of people who did not resonate with it. That's the thing about standing for something—even a belief like "I don't believe in working much during the holidays" can be polarizing. And that's okay! It's good, even! You're looking to attract *your* people.

People are naturally drawn to people who are "like them." In psychology, this is called the similarity-attraction effect. We are all looking for people who align with us in various ways. We choose friends who are similar to us in background and attitude. Sometimes friend groups even end up looking like each other because subconsciously we are drawn to people who dress like us. Yes, there are obvious downsides to this phenomenon, and I'd never suggest living in a silo. But there's an important takeaway for your business: if you are honest and clear about your values, you will attract those who share them. And when we communicate in an authentic way and weave our values into our company, our membership, and everything we do, we create a deeper connection with those we wish to serve.

Now I know that we may not want to be polarizing or we might prefer to avoid conflict. I get that. But if you try to please everyone, you'll ultimately please no one. You will experience *far more* growth if you voice your opinions, beliefs, and philosophies. I'm not suggesting you have to talk about politics or religion (I actually encourage you to stay away from those topics), but I am encouraging you to put thought into the things that are important to you and have the courage to share them. Because in doing so, you're giving voice to the things your audience is naturally thinking, feeling, and even wanting to say. That alignment is a *big* reason they will follow you. So if sharing scares you, start small. Just know that you aren't only doing this for you. It's also for those you wish to lead inside your membership.

In my business, we have a set of core values that guide us in all our endeavors. They are **impact, innovation, integrity, simplicity, community, and fun**. Each of these values is interwoven into everything we do, from our marketing to our customer service. By vocalizing and embodying these values in our social content and inside our membership, we amplify our connection with our audience.

Take a moment and reflect on your own beliefs. Jot down the things that immediately come to mind. If you're having trouble, think about the things you don't like or can't stand. As I learned with good ole Gary Vee, that can be just as helpful.

- What really gets you fired up, in either a positive or negative way?
- What makes you cringe?
- What brings you joy?
- What do you have a strong opinion on?
- What triggers an emotion?
- What do you find yourself debating with others?
- What drives you absolutely bonkers?
- What are you absolutely against?

After you answer these questions, then ask yourself, *Why?* Why do you feel so strongly about these things? Your answers will quickly guide you to the principles you deem important and worth standing for. The reason I immediately became clear that hustle culture was *not* my scene was because business, for me, was about control. Control to do things the way I wanted and how I wanted. And those things boil down to being with the people who matter most. This is why I started pursuing the membership model in the first place.

And if I dig a little deeper into my "why," I realize that some of this comes back to my parents. They didn't have much control over their financial future and had to work jobs they didn't like. They had to work long hours and sacrifice so many of their hopes and dreams because they didn't see an alternative option. But they did this because their ultimate goal was to set up my sister and me with a life where we wouldn't have to worry about those things. That's something I will forever be grateful for and want to honor with the life I've chosen. I want to use that gift, and control over my future, to design the life I want around the business and not the other way around.

When you gain this kind of clarity, lean into it. Take ownership and stand firm in it, even if others disagree. Next, distill each of your values down to short phrases or single words. This will make it easier for you to remember what you stand for and for others to connect with, as well. What values do you hold in the highest regard in your life? This is your superpower for attracting your people.

Here are some ideas to get the juices flowing.

- Acceptance
- Accountability
- Awareness
- Balance
- Bravery
- Cleanliness
- Community
- Compassion
- Confidence
- Consistency
- Creativity
- Credibility
- Dignity
- Discipline
- Drive
- Empathy
- Empowerment
- Energy
- Enthusiasm
- Ethical
- Family
- Focus
- Freedom
- Friendship

- Fun
- Grace
- Gratitude
- Greatness
- Growth
- Happiness
- Hard Work
- Health
- Honesty
- Hope
- Imagination
- Independence
- Individuality
- Joy
- Kindness
- Knowledge
- Leadership
- Learning
- Logic
- Love
- Loyalty
- Maturity
- Motivation
- Order
- Organization
- Originality
- Passion
- Productivity
- Professionalism
- Prosperity
- Purpose
- Recreation
- Respect
- Responsibility
- Risk
- Spirituality
- Spontaneity
- Stability
- Strength
- Structure
- Success
- Support
- Surprise
- Teamwork
- Tolerance
- Toughness
- Traditional
- Tranquility
- Transparency
- Trustworthy
- Truth
- Understanding
- Uniqueness
- Vision
- Vitality
- Wealth

As you begin to build your audience and pick your platform, don't be afraid to stand for something. Take one look at my Instagram feed or e-mails, and you'll see I weave fun into everything. My pictures are always silly; my tone is always informal. I showcase my values by posting about my kids and wife and the things we do together. I'm intentionally attracting the same kinds of people who want the same life. You'll attract the right people to you and experience much faster growth as a result of standing for something.

WHAT DO YOU STAND FOR?

RECREATION TRUTH SPIRITUALITY RESPONSIBILITY
ACCEPTANCE COMPASSION CONSISTENCY CONFIDENCE
ACCOUNTABILITY BRAVERY CLEANLINESS AWARENESS BALANCE COMMUNITY
CREATIVITY CREDIBILITY ETHICAL EMPOWERMENT ENERGY DISCIPLINE DRIVE
ENTHUSIASM DIGNITY SUCCESS TRANSPARENCY VITALITY
FREEDOM FOCUS FAMILY TEAMWORK FRIENDSHIP EMPATHY FUN GRACE
GRATITUDE GROWTH HONESTY HEALTH HARD WORK GREATNESS
HOPE IMAGINATION INDEPENDENCE JOY KINDNESS INDIVIDUALITY HAPPINESS
LEADERSHIP LEARNING KNOWLEDGE LOYALTY MATURITY ORDER PASSION
LOGIC LOVE ORGANIZATION PRODUCTIVITY ORIGINALITY PURPOSE RESPECT
RISK STRENGTH STRUCTURE PROSPERITY STABILITY PROFESSIONALISM
VISION UNIQUENESS WEALTH
TOLERANCE UNDERSTANDING TRADITIONAL TOUGHNESS

CHAPTER 9

PICK ONE PLATFORM TO RULE THEM ALL

To start building an audience, pick a platform.

That's it. That's the chapter.

Okay, I'm halfway kidding. But seriously, that's *mostly* it.

Every day there is a new social media platform or content-sharing site popping up, each with its own unique features and audience. Facebook, Instagram, YouTube, Snapchat, Pinterest, TikTok, LinkedIn, and, of course, Twitter (or "X" . . . whatever Elon is calling it these days). We're going to start by picking just *one* platform. You don't have to be everywhere all at once. In fact, I encourage you *not* to be. **If you try to be in all the places at once, you end up not being anywhere or serving anyone effectively.**

Do a little research to find out where your potential audience likes to hang out and where they are most active and engaged already. Different platforms cater to different audiences. Some prefer the familiarity and community of Facebook, while others are more drawn to the visually driven world of Instagram. Some are captivated by the short, snappy videos on TikTok, while others seek professional networking opportunities on LinkedIn. Do your best to go where your audience already is.

Also consider where *you* feel most comfortable. Do you already know a particular social media app pretty well? Do you like writing long posts or speaking on camera better? Figuring out where your audience naturally hangs out is important, but it's just as important to cater to your own strengths. Trying new things and pushing yourself out of your comfort zone is definitely a part of being an entrepreneur. But at the beginning, when you're just getting started and building momentum, it's beneficial to pick the platform that's easiest and most natural for you.

The important thing here is to not complicate this too much. Make an educated guess. You can always pivot or repurpose your content later to other platforms (we'll cover that in Chapter 12). But it's much easier to make progress if you're already moving forward with momentum. I knew that by focusing my initial efforts on one platform, I would be able to make a bigger impact in a shorter period of time. When I was first starting out, I chose Facebook as my platform. I was familiar with it and I knew a lot of customers in my market were already there as well. Plus, I also knew there was an opportunity (when I was ready) to advertise on that platform. That was a big plus for me. Yours can be as simple as that too. Don't let the thought of picking slow you down. Just choose, get started, and begin creating content to serve your audience!

Here is the six-step process that we're going to follow to attract your audience:

1. **Pick your platform.** Let's say you've done this. Boom.
2. **Create content that showcases your expertise and establishes your authority.** This just means producing valuable and engaging content that captures the attention of your audience. Don't panic. I'll teach you how to do this easily and quickly in the next chapter.
3. **Post consistently.** In order to build trust and credibility, you need to consistently produce content and engage with your audience. This means developing a regular rhythm and schedule for creating and sharing content.

4. **Engage with your audience.** It is vitally important to connect with your audience and build relationships. By actively engaging with those who consume your content, you further establish your authority and create a loyal following.
5. **Open a conversation.** This means to start chatting with your audience in the comments, DMs, e-mail, or on calls.
6. **Generate a sale.** Even if you don't have anything to sell yet, this can just mean getting your audience to sign up for your free list-builder (see Chapter 13).

This method can be applied to basically *every* platform, even with stuff changing constantly. If you're reading this book 50 years after it's published and the hottest social media site is called ToeJammer, this still works. Post on ToeJammer! If you're just starting out and ToeJammer makes sense, start there, but don't try to be everywhere all at once. It's very difficult to do, especially in the beginning. Stack your odds of success; streamline your efforts. These are the fundamentals of what you want to do everywhere, no matter how things advance or change. Do you know why? Because the principles stay the same. And people stay the same.

It's that simple. All you're trying to do is help people and be a cool, normal person. Don't be fake. Don't oversell. Don't be weird. Just relax and meet people where they are. Prescribe a solution that will help them and be of service, and you'll win fans for life.

As you follow these steps, you'll begin to see the snowball effect. Your efforts may start small, but over time, they will grow exponentially. As you continue to pour into your audience and provide valuable content, you will create trust and establish your authority. This will set the stage to make an offer for your membership because your people will already know, like, and trust you.

Now it's time to embark on your audience-building journey. Consider where your audience hangs out, what kind of content they enjoy, and where you can make the biggest impact. Once you've made your choice, you'll turn your focus to creating valuable content, being consistent, and engaging with your audience. And remember, this is an investment of time in your business. Eventually, you want your content to spread far and wide across different formats. And that begins today, by just picking one. So . . . what will your platform be?

You might be thinking, *Okay, Stu, I picked my platform. But now what the heck do I* actually *post?* That's up next, friend. We're going to talk about how to establish yourself as the go-to authority in your market and create a whole bunch of content (the easy way!) that aligns with the topic of your membership.

CHAPTER 10

THE 5-PART FRAMEWORK FOR CREATING ENGAGING CONTENT

As you begin to build your audience, whether by posting on social media or some of the other methods we'll cover later, it helps to have an easy framework to follow every time to make creating content simple. Luckily for you, I created just such a framework and we're going to cover it right now. You can use this anywhere and anytime you're trying to reach potential customers and help them solve a problem. Easy peasy!

Here's my five-part framework for teaching any lesson.

1. **Open with a hook**. You already know the problem that you're going to solve, so the hook should be based around that. Just make it short and snappy, something that instantly gets their attention and lets them know they're in for some incredible value. Base the hook around their problems, challenges, desires, or dream outcome. I also like hooks that create intrigue or tickle their curiosity. If you ever get stuck here, refer to Chapter 14 on headlines.

2. **Move into a story**. It should be clear to you by now how much I love using stories to teach. Stories are memorable and are hands down the absolute best way to connect with people. The story you use could be about you or someone else you know who also experienced the same problem this audience is facing. Foreshadow the fact that there is a solution, a better way, and that you'll be revealing it in a moment.
3. **Deliver the actual lesson**. Get clear about the purpose behind what you're about to share. Lay out the bullet points of exactly how to solve the problem. My recommendation is to keep your takeaways to a minimum. I generally have three to five per lesson. I've found if there are more than that, people get overwhelmed and don't end up doing anything with what is shared. To quote comedian Ken Davis from his speaker training called SCORRE™, "What do you want your audience to know or do as a result of your presentation?"
4. **Make a call to action**. This is the all-important part of your presentation where you want to instruct people to go to your landing page so they can get one of your amazing list-builders. To really sweeten the pot here, I encourage you to create a list-builder specifically for the audience you're teaching. It might be a little extra work, but it's really worth it. Amy could create a one-sheet that had a list of websites and resources where people could buy the towels, linens, and other touches that she uses to create the five-star experience. It wouldn't take too long and could be extremely targeted to that exact audience and presentation. This type of answer guide is easy to transition to at the end of a presentation. Typically I would say something like, "Chances are, you may still have questions about how to start a membership site. The good news is I've put together a guide answering the top 10 questions I get asked about launching and growing a membership. Plus, I've loaded it with *tons* of real-world examples that will definitely get your creative juices flowing. If you'd

like it, just go to www.TheMembershipGuide.com." Simple, right? What you don't want to do is have a completely irrelevant list-builder. It needs to be in alignment with what you just taught.

5. **Offer a quick summary of everything you just taught and reinforce the call to action.** Tie it up in a nice little bow. I always end with something like, "So today we talked about [HOOK]. We covered [Lesson 1], [Lesson 2], and [Lesson 3]. And if you'd like the free guide guaranteed to answer your most pressing questions about starting a membership as well as get your creative juices flowing about *your* membership, go to www.TheMembershipGuide.com."

Here's an example of this in action. Our community member Blake Fly was asked to emcee a large virtual event. Normally he would charge a flat fee for it, but in this case, I suggested he forego his fee in exchange for being able to offer the audience a free resource that would help them implement some teaching from the event.

So that's exactly what he did. At some point in the conference he took 10 minutes to do a quick lesson on how to connect with people you don't know, and at the end he told people that if they'd like more strategies, to head to a URL and get some free ideas. This was his list-builder, of course, one that he'd created just for this event and audience.

In just 10 minutes of delivering a quick lesson with a specific CTA, he added over 400 people to his e-mail list! These were highly targeted people who had shown they invested themselves by already paying over $2,000 to be a part of the event! That's how powerful this can be. Oh, and as a bonus, emceeing this event led to sales, additional speaking gigs, and all kinds of other opportunities.

With this framework in your back pocket, you'll be able to whip up content and lessons for your audience whenever you need to. You can also lengthen it to use it for webinars, live videos, or any kind of teaching. Now let's get into how to plan out months worth of posts in just a few hours.

CHAPTER 11

CREATE 30 DAYS OF CONTENT WITH ONE SIMPLE SYSTEM

Creating content that attracts your ideal clients doesn't have to be complicated or overly time-consuming! It can be easy and fast. So easy and fast, in fact, that you can map out the content for your platform in a matter of minutes. Are you ready?

I'm going to teach you a little framework that we use to produce a whole lot of content in a short period of time. When I walk you through this, it might actually feel almost too simple. I want you to put aside any judgments or preconceived notions. Just embrace this idea and be open to the simplicity of the framework.

Before we get into it, I want you to flex those research muscles that you built in Chapter 9 and dive into some Facebook groups, comments on blog posts, or YouTube videos, etc. that are around the subject matter of your membership. Reference your Messaging Map again. Because we are (always!) looking for the **problems** and **challenges** that your market is facing. Remember, platform-building is just helping people. So let's help our people with their problems.

When you're scanning through the different Facebook groups, blog post comments, YouTube videos, or whatever social media, look for frustrations. Look for the language that indicates that people want something, but they don't have it yet. Language like "I wish somebody could help me with _______." "Does anybody know how to do ________?" "I'm frustrated by ________." Those types of things. You're looking for language of frustration, challenges, and questions that come up over and over again.

For example, my wife set up a luxury Airbnb property, and she's had tremendous success with it. So much so that we charge three times the average nightly rate for our area. It's booked solid all the time. She also gets five-star reviews, rebookings, and referrals like clockwork (you can find it on Instagram @DoverLakeHouse). Inevitably we've had a lot of people who have asked Amy, "How did you do this? I'd love to be able to do something similar." One of Amy's secrets is that she focuses heavily on the "experience," which enables her to charge a lot more. This is the *big* reason why people keep coming back. Everything Amy does to shape the guest experience is intentional. There is a repeatable process. And as these questions come her way, she has been freely answering whoever has asked.

Being the membership guy, one day I said to her, "Babes, this would make for a great membership."

And she said, "What do you mean?"

I said, "Well, you could teach other people how to do this."

She replied, "Oh, but you know, it's pretty straightforward and simple."

Time-out. **If you've ever gone down that path where you've thought, *Oh, this is simple—everybody knows this.* Let me tell you right now: no, they don't.** This is why you want to pay attention to these kinds of clues. When people are asking you questions or you see them trying to find answers in groups or discussion forums, these are clues to potential problems and challenges that the market is facing. What might seem easy and effortless for you can be difficult or challenging for them.

To start, Amy didn't have an audience of people interested in creating luxury Airbnb experiences. So we went on Facebook and checked out a few groups. All I did was search for groups related to "short-term rentals" or "Airbnb." Very quickly I found several groups, some with tens of thousands of people—a few even had hundreds of thousands of people! Then I started scanning through these groups and doing exactly what I'm suggesting you do, looking for problems and challenges. Within two minutes of scanning one of the Facebook groups, I found a common problem that kept coming up. People were asking, "What is everybody doing for bedsheets and linens? Are you using color bedsheets or white bedsheets? What about kids' sheets? Are you using white for those? And what about towels? Are you guys buying expensive towels?"

> ***You're going to see that there's an endless number of ideas for content.***

I asked Amy and she said, " I just go to this particular store and I buy this brand." I stopped her, "Yeah, but *why* do you buy that brand?" I asked. It was obvious to her what the answer was, but clearly not so obvious to everyone else. As it turned out, Amy had answers like this for everything. She knew what candles to buy, what snacks people love, and how to arrange decorations that immediately got people taking pictures and sharing them on social media. And most importantly relative to this discussion, she knew exactly what linens and towels people love—so much so that they were mentioning them in their actual reviews of our Airbnb!

The same is true for you in your market. If you start doing some research, you're going to see that there's an endless number of ideas for content. This will provide the foundation for our framework for producing content the easy way. From your research, brainstorm as many different problems, challenges, and questions as you can imagine. Keep writing them down, stream-of-consciousness style. Don't think too much about it. Don't overanalyze it. Just keep writing them down. If you find yourself thinking, *Yeah, but this is kind of the same thing,* I don't care right now. Just write. Collect as many as possible because I'm going to have you plug them into something I call the 10 x 3 Framework. And if you're having trouble coming up with some, hang on, because in Chapter 12 I'll show you a shortcut to all of this.

The concept is simple. Find 10 different problems or challenges. My guess is that in your research, you're going to find a heck of a lot more than that. But for this exercise, all we're looking for is 10. Then what you're going to do is provide 3 solutions, or strategies, for each of these 10 problems. And guess what happens? You now have 30 days' worth of content just like that. Badda bing, badda boom. Easy peasy, pudding, and pie. And you can repeat this process as many times as you need. You could map out months, or even a year's worth, of content in just a few hours.

Our student Lisa K. is an intuition coach and runs a membership helping others better connect with divine guidance. If you take a look at her Instagram page, you'll see she's doing the 10 x 3 Framework perfectly. You'll find posts like "5 clear ways to tell the difference between intuition and fear" and "3 steps to call your guardian angel for help." She's mapped out her content with solutions to many of the questions and challenges she knows her audience has.

Really, that's it. All you're doing is looking for 10 different problems and providing 3 possible solutions (tips, ideas, strategies, tools, resources, or even useful websites, books, podcasts, videos, etc.) for each one. Remember when I told you to set aside your doubts and just trust me on this one? It really is that easy. So, as my friend Susie Moore says, "Let it be easy!" Remember, stress-free is part of the philosophy. For more examples of what this can look like for certain niches, head to predictableprofitsbook.com.

The bottom line is that you always start by creating content for one platform and focusing on problems and challenges that your market faces. What's creating difficulty for them? Where is there friction or tension? What is keeping them up at night? What questions do they have, and what are they asking over and over and over again?

If you do this consistently, you will become the go-to person in your subject area and eventually have success stories you can share. Years ago, before we developed my course, I was running WishList Member, and it was the world's number one membership plug-in for WordPress. We were serving tens of thousands of people. Then, like I mentioned before, I sold my shares.

After that, I really wasn't sure what I was going to do. On the one hand I was confident in myself and knew that creating space was what I needed to discover my next thing. But on the other hand, I felt this huge sense of urgency that whatever it was going to be, I needed to figure it out fast—especially because I had just become a father. So I proactively reached out to friends and colleagues and asked their thoughts. One day, one of my dear friends and mentors, Reid Tracy, said to me, "You know, Stu, you should just really focus on helping people grow thriving and profitable membership sites."

"But I don't know if there's enough people that really want to learn or utilize this," I said.

And Reid kindly replied, "I think you're wrong, and I really want to encourage you to go in this direction." Reid had been in business way longer than I had. He's the CEO of Hay House (the company that actually published this book!) and in my opinion, he is infinitely more wise than I will ever be. So I decided to trust his encouragement. I set aside my own judgment and listened to him. Has that ever happened to you? Where someone gave you a piece of advice that you felt hesitant about but you trusted them, and likely knew deep in your gut that they were right?

But then I started to wonder, *How am I going to establish my authority in this space*? I had built WishList, but I was hardly publicly known as a "membership expert." I was more of a behind-the-scenes guy. So, like you, I had to start building a platform from scratch to build my audience. First, I picked my platform. Then I had to create some content, and I wasn't sure what to do since I had never created any "front-facing" content before. My brother-in-law and business partner, Andrew, said to me, "Stu, as long as I've known you, you've never had a problem talking. We just need to get you talking about the topics that our people are interested in and the problems and challenges that they're facing."

So that's exactly what we did. We started hunting for problems, questions, and challenges that people had about how to take what they knew and turn it into a recurring revenue membership. I knew how to solve those problems. It's what I had been doing for years. I just hadn't ever taught it publicly. So I used the 10 x 3 Framework that I just outlined for you. And at the end of each video, I asked, "P.S., do you have a question about growing a profitable membership? Let me know in the comments."

What happened was I started to get *tons* of questions. And they created the basis for an endless number of ideas that we could produce. I didn't have to struggle or squeeze any ideas out of my brain because they were coming to me effortlessly. I simply answered the questions people were asking to produce content consistently and easily. You can do the same thing.

Bonus tip: If you have an e-mail newsletter, add a little "P.S." at the end of your first e-mail after someone subscribes. Simply ask them, "What's your biggest challenge with [OUTCOME THEY DESIRE]? Hit reply and let me know!" Mine was, "What's your biggest challenge with growing a profitable membership site? Hit reply and let me know!"

Start with your research and implement the 10 x 3 Framework. And when you add the little bonus tip that I gave you about asking your audience for more of their questions, you're going to get tons of new questions coming to you regularly. From that point forward, it's just about answering those questions.

In the meantime, not only are you creating content consistently and being extremely helpful to your ideal customers, but you're establishing your authority in your market. That's exactly what happened to me. It wasn't long before anybody who had a question about memberships was saying, "Oh, you have to go talk to Stu"—all from growing my audience from scratch, using this exact framework, and posting on just one platform.

Real talk: I know you're probably thinking, *Stu, creating all of this content sounds like a lot of work*. And although it's well worth it, you're right—it is going to take you time to create it. And in the next chapter, we're going to talk about how to create a whole lot of content *really* fast.

> At predictableprofitsbook.com, I've created a free downloadable template to help you create your own content calendar based on the problem/solution framework.

CHAPTER 12

CONTENT CREATION TRICKS TO PRODUCE MORE, FASTER

I know you're busy. You have a life and kids and a job or a business and don't have the time to spend hours every day coming up with what to post on social media or what content you're going to create next. This chapter provides a list of tips for creating content in a fast and easy way.

1. BATCH PRODUCE.

Basically, create a bunch of content all at once. I encourage you to schedule specific days for creating content in bulk. Let me give you an example.

One day, when we were addressing these problem/solution frameworks with our team, Rick, our marketing director, suggested carving out an afternoon for me to answer a bunch of questions related to membership sites. We blocked out three hours for this. The process was simple: Rick asked me questions off-camera, and I answered them one after the other while the camera was focused on me. This resulted in a wealth of content (tons of short videos) that we could then schedule. The same approach can work for you too. Try to think about creating content for two or three months at a time, providing you with a buffer and enough breathing room to engage with your audience effectively. Do it once, and focus on something else.

2. HAVE SOMEONE OFF-CAMERA ASK YOU QUESTIONS TO MAKE THE PROCESS FEEL MORE NATURAL AND FLUID.

If you don't have someone physically present, you can use a Zoom meeting and record the conversation. There are lots of ways to achieve this, and the details of how you implement it aren't nearly as important as just actually doing it. It's essential to maximize your efficiency.

Pro tip: After someone asks you the question off-camera, repeat it in your response. So for example, if someone asked me, "What's the most effective way to boost retention?" I would respond with, "The most effective way to boost retention is . . ." and then I'd go into my response. Make sense? Doing this means your videos aren't dependent on the "question" being in the video, and it speeds up the process when publishing that content.

3. PRODUCE CONTENT IN MULTIPLE FORMATS.

But hold on now, Stu. You told me I only had to pick one platform! That's true, but hear me out. You don't have to create any more content than just what you've done with the 10 x 3 Framework. For example, if you create video content, use tools to automatically generate audio versions and transcripts. They do the heavy lifting. This way, you can cater to different audience preferences and expand your reach effectively. One piece of content can become a video clip, audio clip, and even posts and captions with the transcripts. Work smarter, not harder, friends.

4. MAKE BITE-SIZED CHUNKS OF CONTENT.

Shorter, easily digestible content keeps people engaged and interested. Your audience will get into the content a lot easier if you have five 10-minute videos vs. one 60-minute video. You want them to be able to finish consuming your content in just a few minutes and walk away with a quick win, something actionable to *do*, or something inspiring to think about. If you can answer people's questions and help them make progress faster and easier, the better it will be!

5. ENSURE THAT YOUR CONTENT REMAINS EVERGREEN.

Avoid referencing specific dates or time-sensitive events that can quickly make your content feel outdated. Focus on principles and concepts that are timeless. You want this content to work for your audience for years. If you reference a worldwide event that happened "yesterday" in your video and a potential customer is watching it two years later, they'll assume the content isn't relevant anymore, even if it is.

6. DON'T OVERLOOK THE VALUE OF REPURPOSING CONTENT.

You likely already have a repository of great content that you can refresh with new examples, insights, or stories. The base of the lesson can remain the same while you present it in different formats or mediums. You can turn the audio of a video into a podcast episode and then take the transcripts and turn that into a blog post and/or captions for an Instagram post. Then take the most interesting snippet of the video and make a TikTok. We use software to help us quickly turn video content into short-form content perfect for platforms like Instagram, Facebook, LinkedIn, and X, as well as for things like a podcast or blog. For example, a few years back, I had a series where I regularly interviewed a member who had done something innovative with their launch. For one of these videos, I interviewed Anna Saucier, who did one of the most remarkable things to launch her membership. (See Chapter 16!) We took that one interview and created a PDF guide for how to launch like Anna, an MP3, a full 31-page transcript, a launch blueprint, a social media script, and an e-mail template. Talk about getting as much use as we can out of one piece of content!

7. REPOST, REPOST, REPOST.

Social media platforms will never show your content to 100 percent of the people who are following you. So when you find a post that resonates, post it again—exactly as you did the first time! Just space it out 30 days into the future. Not everyone sees your content and not everyone remembers it. And as I write this chapter and look at my Instagram feed, I can tell you that one reel I posted two days ago has almost as many views, more comments, and about half as many "saves" as it did when I originally posted it over 30 days ago. So when you find a winner, keep it in a library of your go-to posts and consistently reuse it. Think about it like this: you're U2, and instead of people coming to your concert and only playing new songs, you keep giving them what they want—the hits! Can you imagine going to a U2 concert and not hearing "Beautiful Day"?

8. USE AI.

Artificial intelligence is the quickest of all ways to create content. You can use AI for all kinds of things, including coming up with content ideas, hooks, and captions. Try out the prompts below on your AI platform of choice:

1. Can you please share 10 main categories for [the topic]?
2. Can you now please help me generate [X] number of ideas for the first category? I'd like to focus on common problems, challenges, fears, desires, goals, or questions people have. I'd like to include a short, curiosity-driven hook, followed by a subheadline that gives a little more context.
3. Can you please provide 3 talking points for each idea in the [topic] category?

Now, like I said before, producing platform content is only part of the puzzle. It allows us to attract an audience (which is good), but we don't own the platform (which is bad). That puts us in a potentially vulnerable situation where our business could be dependent on something we have very little control over. The good news is that there is a very viable solution that works in concert with building your platform audience—and that's building your e-mail list. In the upcoming chapters, we'll talk through how to move people from your social platforms to your e-mail list.

TURN ONE PIECE of CONTENT into
BLUE PRINT
GUIDES
POD CAST
BLOG POST
YOUTUBE VIDEO
SLIDES
EMAIL TEMPLATE
#
SOCIAL MEDIA POSTS

CHAPTER 13

TWO POWERFUL IDEAS THAT GENERATED OVER 100K LEADS

All right my friend, it's time to focus on building your e-mail list, which is the most valuable asset for your business. **Here's the truth: the bigger the list, the more money you're going to make.** And everybody wants that, right? Unlike social media platforms that can be shut down or accounts that can be closed, an e-mail list is something we own and can use to directly communicate with our audience. One of my friends, Shaa Wasmund, had her Facebook account hacked. And unfortunately, the hacker started producing inappropriate content, and so Facebook completely shut down her account. And then they also shut down her Instagram.

Imagine that . . . you're serving your audience every day with valuable content and then all of a sudden, because of something completely out of your control, your accounts are shut down. It took Shaa months of trying to get in touch with somebody who could help. To make matters worse, because she didn't have access to her account, she also couldn't run any ads. It was a nightmare. But because she had an e-mail list, she was able to keep her business running and generate sales for her courses. Hopefully, this never happens to you, but if it does, you want to be prepared.

To grow a business successfully, we need to focus on three areas: getting attention (we covered this!), converting that attention (either to our e-mail list or a sale), and keeping attention (retaining customers, which we'll cover in Chapter 41). Right now, we'll concentrate on converting attention from our platform to our e-mail list. One of the ways we do that is by creating a list-builder: something you offer your audience for free in exchange for them giving you their e-mail address.

The primary goal of a list-builder is to provide value upfront and build a strong relationship with the audience. This will nurture the connection with them, making it easier to make offers later on. You won't have to work as hard to make the sale because that relationship (know, like, and trust) was built early on. A good list-builder does a couple of things.

1. **It should solve a specific problem and offer a clear benefit to the audience.** It's essential that it leads to a quick win, as instant gratification is highly attractive. For example, if you have knee pain and you came across a PDF that outlines exactly how to reduce it in three easy steps, that's going to be pretty compelling for you. On the contrary, another download that just talks about the general idea of pain in our bodies would be way less interesting. Be as clear as you can about the benefit of your list-builder and as specific as possible about the problem you solve.
2. **It should position you as the expert in your market.** Not only should it provide great value, but it should increase the likelihood of somebody wanting to work with you inside your membership.

There are three main categories of list-builders, defined by what they help your audience achieve: growing (intellectually, emotionally, or spiritually), saving (time, money, or effort), and educating (providing templates, resources, etc.). From these categories, you can create compelling and valuable list-builders.

Here is a list to get your creative juices flowing:

1. Checklist—a simple, actionable list
2. E-book—a longer, in-depth guide
3. Infographic—a visual representation
4. Webinar—an online seminar or workshop
5. Mini-course—a shortened course
6. Template—a pre-made document or file
7. Tool kit—a collection of resources, tools, or apps
8. Quiz—an interactive way for users to gain insights
9. Cheat sheet—a concise set of notes or pointers
10. Case study—a detailed analysis of a particular project
11. Free trial—a limited-time access to a product
12. Discount coupon—a special offer
13. Exclusive video content—premium video material
14. Challenge—a step-by-step series of tasks or prompts
15. Resource list—a curated list of useful tools
16. Calculator or tool—an interactive tool
17. Swipe file—a collection of tested and proven marketing e-mails, templates, copy for webpages, etc.
18. Behind-the-scenes look—exclusive content
19. Event tickets—free or discounted passes
20. Expert interview—an in-depth conversation

As you can see, there are many things you can do. But for our purposes of getting you going as quickly as possible, I'd like to go a little deeper with two of the most effective list builders that have generated hundreds of thousands of leads for our business. And best of all, they've passed the test of time because they have consistently generated us leads for more than five years! The two that I'm referring to are the curated PDF and the answer guide. These are both fast and easy to create and check all the boxes of what makes a great list-builder. The good news is, if you've done your homework from the previous chapters, then you're way ahead of things. You'll be able to use all of that material to create your own freebies.

THE CURATED PDF

This is a simple but *very* effective list-builder that your audience will love. It involves reaching out to experts or clients and asking them specific questions related to your market. Then you curate their responses and add your own insights.

I first discovered the curated PDF when I was working with Michael Hyatt. We were in the process of creating a new program called "Five Days to Your Best Year Ever," but we lacked an audience that would be the perfect fit for the program. We had to build one. After brainstorming with the team, Megan, Michael's eldest daughter, came up with an idea.

She suggested reaching out to various experts and asking them about their year-end preparation rituals for the upcoming new year. It was a brilliant idea! Michael began reaching out to his friends and colleagues, and we gathered their responses. They came in various forms—videos, audio, and written replies. We meticulously curated these responses, identifying common themes and organizing them accordingly. Michael added his own commentary and insights based on the shared responses. Remarkably, from concept to completion, this process took just a few days.

I implemented this same strategy into my business years later, but instead of reaching out to other experts in the field, I reached out to my own mastermind members and asked them all one question: What is the most effective way you've grown your membership in the last 12 months? Pretty great question, right? Everyone else thought so too, as it's been a super effective list-builder for us. By the way, you can find it at predictableprofitsbook.com if you're curious.

A third example of this was when we created the "World's Shortest Marketing Conference." It was a fun twist on this idea. Instead of it being a PDF, we asked everyone to give their best marketing tip in 60 seconds or less. Then we compiled the tips into a members area using Membership.io. That process took us a total of two hours. The most time-consuming part was collecting the videos. But when it was finished, we had a list-builder that our audience *loved* and one that has been very effective in helping us build our e-mail list. (You can see this list at www.60MarketingIdeas.com.)

What was even more exciting about each of these curated list-builders was that each of these simple ideas helped us amass an audience of tens of thousands, all ideal customers for the program we were offering. We did the effort once. And for years since, we continue to use them as a tool in building our list. The point is that by tapping into the collective wisdom of others and curating it, you can generate a valuable resource and list-builder.

Pro tip: When you collect responses for your curated PDF, you've also instantly created a whole bunch of social media content. Each response can be used as its own social post with a call to action of "Get more ideas like this at www.YourURL.com."

There are two main approaches to implementing this strategy:

1. **Engaging Established Experts**: Connect with well-known figures in your field, even if you don't have a prior relationship with them. Gather their insights on a specific question related to your audience, and then curate them.
2. **Leveraging Existing Clients or Customers**: Ask your current clients, customers, or members the same question. Their firsthand experiences can provide valuable insights.

After you decide who you're going to approach for responses, follow these steps:

1. **Define the Question**: Determine a question that your audience is eager to have answered. Look to the research you've done, considering your audience's problems, challenges, or curiosities.
2. **Reach Out to Contributors**: If you're involving established experts, compile a list and start contacting them. Make the process easy for them, allowing them to respond in their preferred format—video, audio, or text. And you're not looking for lengthy responses. Many times, shorter is better. Usually two to three minutes is plenty.
3. **Curate the Responses**: As the responses come in, identify common themes and patterns. Organize the content in a logical manner. Remember to get their permission to quote them and use their ideas in this way.
4. **Add Your Insights**: Share your overarching insights and reflections on the collected responses. Highlight commonalities and valuable takeaways.

This is a strategy that you can take action on right now. A huge benefit is you don't even need to create a ton of content on your own. You can leverage the wisdom of others.

You can find some bonus curated PDFs to use as inspiration at preditableprofitsbook.com.

THE ANSWER GUIDE

The answer guide is equally as straightforward and dependent on a lot of the research you've already done. But for this one, you don't need to reach out to anyone. In fact, I bet you could get a rough version of this complete within a day. All it involves is answering the top 10 questions you frequently get asked or find in your research.

You can record video responses to these questions, transcribe your responses, and then turn them into a PDF guide. You've now got another highly valuable resource for your audience.

Have you noticed yet that what we're doing here is usually just building on things that we've already done in the past? I'm all about simplicity. And since you've already done so much great market research, there's no reason to reinvent the wheel.

My team and I came to discover the answer guide list-builder simply because we were getting frustrated that we got the same questions over and over again. My team constantly said, "Hey, Stu, I'm sorry, I know you've answered this a million times, but the community is asking about __________ again." So one day we (you guessed it) blocked out a few hours to batch-answer our FAQs. Rick asked the questions off-camera again, and we ripped right through them. Then we used Membership.io to create transcripts to create an answer guide.

Everything I'm teaching you here is exactly what I did to build my audience and exactly what we still do today. It may almost feel too simple, but don't discount the idea because the answer guide has helped us welcome hundreds of thousands of people into our world. And we use it virtually every single week each time we see a question in our free Facebook group. We direct people to it by saying, "This is a great question. I answered this as well as nine other top questions we get asked about launching and growing a profitable membership site. You can find all my answers and ideas by going to www.TheMembershipGuide.com."

You better believe we used video clips of me answering those questions on social media, and at the end of each one we mentioned that people could go to TheMembershipGuide.com to download the ultimate answer guide about memberships. And since we kept it evergreen and didn't say anything to date the material, we've used this same list-builder for years.

Here's a recap of the steps to the answer guide:

1. Collect or assemble 10 questions that your market wants to know the answers to.
2. Answer those questions. I always recommend doing this via video so you can repurpose the content in multiple ways. Don't worry if you're not great on camera. It doesn't have to be perfect.
3. Take the transcripts of your responses, add them into a document, and sprinkle in any examples that would support what you shared. You don't need fancy graphics or branding. You can add any of that later if you want.

Both the curated PDF and answer guide are very simple list-builders that you can create now as assets that are going to help you grow your business every day. Even if you are a seasoned business owner, these aren't too simple for you to use. Every year my team and I still use these exact formats to grow our list, especially before a big launch.

Next, we're going to walk through the steps of creating a landing page that is going to attract the people you want in your membership. I'll show you how to increase your e-mail conversions by doing just a few simple things.

CHAPTER 14

YOUR GUIDE TO A LANDING PAGE THAT CONVERTS

Once you have your list-builder ready to go, you need a landing page. This is simply where people enter their name and e-mail to join your list. What you want is for a high percentage of people who land on your landing page to end up entering their e-mail address to get your list-builder, making for a good conversion.

A stellar landing page should clearly communicate three key elements.

1. **The problem your audience is facing.** People respond when they see a solution to their problem, so being overt about the issue is essential.
2. **How your list-builder will help solve that problem.** If you have an answer guide that aids in progress and success, make sure to communicate that outright.
3. **The benefits that come with solving the problem.** Show how people's lives will improve or become easier once they have the solution. It's essential to convey what possibilities will open up for them once they experience the benefits.

These three elements should be conveyed through four functional components: a headline, a sub-headline, a call-to-action

(CTA) button, and an image. The headline is the most critical part, as it directly speaks to the problem your list builder solves. The subheadline provides a little further context and explanation. Next, we have the CTA button, which you want people to click to get the list-builder. It's crucial this is clear and persuasive. Then the image adds visual appeal and can help support your message.

Whatever software solution you wish to use will have great tutorials on how to set up these pages. The software you pick will largely depend on your budget, experience, and goals. But at the very least, just search "How to set up a landing page" or use our easy guide here.

But here's the biggest takeaway from this chapter: you can get everything else wrong about your landing page, but if you get the headline right, you'll still be in a great shape. Why? No one will ever click to get your list-builder if they don't see something valuable that they want in the headline. Nail the headline, and list-building becomes much easier. You do this by following one basic rule: **BE SPECIFIC.**

You have your Messaging Map and have done your research. You know what problems your audience is facing. Now it's time to speak to them *specifically*. Here's an example of two headlines I wrote for free resources.

Version 1: My Top Secrets to Grow Your Membership

Version 2: How to Eliminate Content Overwhelm
Inside Your Membership

Do you see the difference? "Top secrets" is good, but it's not very specific. It doesn't say exactly what problem it will solve and leaves a lot to the imagination. It doesn't evoke any kind of reaction. On the other hand, "Eliminate content overwhelm" speaks to a very specific problem membership site owners experience. Their members have been overwhelmed with the amount of content, and so have they! This hits harder because it identifies a definitive problem and promises a clear solution.

Another way to write compelling, specific headlines is to call out a pain point that your customers have. Here's another example of two headlines.

> Version 1: Do These 3 Things to Boost Retention
>
> Version 2: Members Canceling? Try This.

In this case, version 1 isn't bad. But version 2 *hurts*. It calls out a pain point, which can add a little juice to your engagement because it elicits that emotional reaction. Membership site owners don't want cancellations. It feels terrible! If you can name a specific ache or irritation that your customers experience, you'll definitely get their attention.

Here's another example:

> Version 1: You Need to Save This ChatGPT Prompt
>
> Version 2: ChatGPT Prompts Every Course or Membership Site Owner Should Use

Version 1 is too broad. Version 2 gets specific about *who* these prompts are for, instantly appealing more to the people we're trying to serve.

Here are a few quick tips on headline writing to make your landing pages convert as effectively as possible.

- Incorporate strong verbs that encourage readers to take action or engage with your content. For example, use words like "Discover," "Learn," "Boost," "Master," or "Unlock."
- Short headlines are more effective because they're easier to digest. Aim for 6 to 8 words, but if necessary, extend to 10 to 12 words max.
- Encourage readers to act by emphasizing time sensitivity. Use phrases like "Limited Time Offer," "Now," or "Last Chance."

- Ask a relevant question to pique readers' curiosity and encourage them to explore your content for answers.
- Incorporate specific numbers in your headline (e.g., "7 Tips" or "10 Ways") to help make your content seem more structured and appealing.
- Explain what readers will gain from your content. Focus on solving a problem or fulfilling a need for them.
- Appeal to readers' emotions with words that trigger feelings or curiosity, such as "Amazing," "Inspiring," "Secrets," or "Surprising."
- Don't be afraid to experiment with different headlines. A/B testing can help you determine which headlines perform best with your audience.
- Avoid clickbait tactics that promise something in the headline but don't deliver in the content. Building trust with your audience is crucial.

When it comes to writing a great headline, there are some proven templates that will set you up for success.

Go to predictableprofitsbook.com for a bunch of free resources, including free templates.

If you still find yourself stuck when it comes to writing headlines, then grab the templates from the online book resources, toss them into any AI writing tool, and ask AI to simply adapt them for your market. You'll have a whole bunch of options ready to go.

Now let's talk about the rest of the landing page. People should be able to see the headline, sub-headline, CTA button, and image immediately without scrolling at all. It should be "above the fold," if you will. You want to grab them quickly. Pay close attention to the wording you use in these elements, as it directly influences the action people take on the page. The words are more important than any image or colors you choose to use. The language in your headline, sub-headline, and CTA button should be action-oriented words that speak to the problem your customer is experiencing and how your free gift solves it.

The biggest mistake that people make is thinking they need these huge, fancy pages with lots of bells and whistles. You don't. In fact, some of our highest-performing landing pages have just been a headline and sub-headline with the CTA button. Keep it simple and avoid overcomplicating your landing page. With an optimized landing page, you'll attract more subscribers to your list and ultimately grow your membership. See some more examples of awesome, simple, high-converting landing pages in the resource section.

Now you've got your foundation set to really begin building your audience. But how do you get traffic to your landing page? In the next chapter, I'm going to show you one simple strategy that has proven to be uber effective.

CHAPTER 15

BORROWED INFLUENCE: THE SECRET BEHIND RAPID LIST GROWTH

One of the best ways to grow your audience is to borrow somebody else's. That's right, you can use the audience somebody else already built to grow your membership or audience. It's one of the secrets to rapidly growing your own e-mail list. You're literally going to slipstream yourself in front of other established audiences in your target market, provide a ton of value, and then lead them to your own list-builder. Here's how.

First, you're going to make three different lists: hot, warm, and cold. Your hot list is anyone who you already have a relationship with. If you don't have an established business already, this list might be short, and that's completely fine. Over time, it will get longer and longer as you build relationships and make new friends in your space. Plenty of people in the warm and cold lists will get moved to the hot over time. They might even become some of your best friends!

On your warm list are people you've connected with at some point but aren't chatting with on the regular. You might have crossed paths at a conference or event, or you might be in some of the same groups or courses like The Membership Experience. You know each other's names and have a few people in common, but you don't talk often. Are there people who come to mind as you read this? Write them down to start creating your warm list.

Next up is your cold list, which are people who have no idea who you are. The cold list has two buckets: obvious and not obvious. The people in the obvious bucket are the ones with a huge audience, where almost anyone interested in your niche knows who they are. For digital entrepreneurship, this list would include people like Amy Porterfield, Jenna Kutcher, Pat Flynn, and Lewis Howes.

For the not-obvious bucket, you're going to fill it by doing exactly what you did in Chapter 6 when you did research to discover your market's hot-button issues to find more people serving your niche.

Come up with a list of topics that people are searching for related to your membership. We're going to use this to find others already serving the same audience. In my case, this might look like "membership," "retention," "subscription," or "community-building." Then combine those words the same way we did in Chapter 2 with places where those audiences might be: Facebook groups, YouTube channels, podcasts, Instagram, TikTok, etc.

For me, this would look like "membership Facebook group," "membership Instagram account," and "membership YouTube channel." You should be able to find dozens, if not hundreds, of other people serving your same audience in a matter of minutes. These go in the not-obvious bucket because you are likely coming across them for the first time in this research. They might have very successful businesses, but they aren't as visible as the *big* ones.

Pay special attention here to the ads that come up when you search each of your keyword terms. Anyone who ranks high in your Google search or is paying for Google ads for these keywords is likely getting a ton of traffic, AKA, tons of your ideal clients. Back in the day when I was an affiliate manager, this is the exact thing I would do to find hundreds of affiliate partners for my clients.

Once you have your four lists with hopefully hundreds of potential partners—hot, warm, cold obvious, and cold not obvious—your next question might be, "Okay, great, Stu, but how do I get these people to want to work with me?"

First of all, give yourself the benefit of the doubt. It's natural for you to be hesitant to reach out. It's normal to worry what the other person will think and how disappointed you may be if they say no. But you and I aren't here to get wrapped up in all of that. At the end of the day, our main goal is to serve people in the highest possible way. So it doesn't really matter if you get a yes or no. It's just a process we're working through. Sometimes when we put out a request and someone says no, it doesn't mean they're saying no as in "they never want to do anything with you ever again." The timing just might be off, and that's okay. Building a membership is a long game.

> ***Our main goal is to serve people in the highest possible way.***

For example, I invited Jenna Kutcher to join me for an online event we hosted as a fundraiser for our charity. It's something we host at the end of every year. The first time I reached out to her, we knew of each other but hadn't really talked (so she was on my warm list). That year, there was a conflict with her schedule, so she passed. The next year, we saw each other backstage at a speaking engagement and we got to hang out a little. I asked again. Unfortunately, she couldn't join us live, but she offered to pre-record a video so that she could be part of it virtually. Then the following year I invited her again. And guess what? We finally made it happen! It was awesome, and we had such a great time and raised a whole lot of money for our charity. We've gone on to become great pals.

But what if I had just stopped after the first no? Remember, the best way to approach someone who already has a following or membership is to do something awesome for *their* audience. You are coming with intentions to serve.

Secondly, and perhaps most importantly, *be cool*. Like, just be cool. If somebody says no (and they will), don't get upset or be uptight about it. They're not saying no because they don't like you. It's almost never personal, so don't internalize it and think that they're saying no because they don't like you. More often it's a conflict of schedule or they have something else at that particular time that's of higher importance. I cannot tell you how many times I've been turned down in my career—*hundreds* probably. But if you just remain cool and act like a nice, normal person, it doesn't matter. And in many cases, another opportunity might work out with that person in the future—even if it takes 2, 3, or even 10 times!

Years ago I used this same strategy when I was hosting my very first seminar. With four weeks to go, I had more speakers scheduled than I had attendees signed up. If you've never hosted a seminar, that's not a good position to be in. I don't know about you, but I happen to get the most creative when I'm most desperate. So I made a list of everybody who was already in front of the audience that I wanted to serve, exactly like I'm telling you here. One of the people on that list was a guy named David Frey. Now, we're great friends. In fact, David even sits on the board of our charity. But back in the day, he had no idea who I was. I reached out to him and we ended up on the phone. Then I requested that he join the promotion for my seminar.

"Stu, that sounds great, but it's not the best timing for my business," he said. I could tell in both his tone and his words that he wasn't interested even though I had walked him through all the benefits and all the amazing ways I was going to serve his audience. I even created a custom landing page and e-mails just for his audience. Still he said no.

I was super disappointed. *But* I stayed cool. "No worries," I said. "Thanks for your time. Oh, and have fun on your trip to Mexico."

"What?" he replied.

"I'm a customer of yours and on your e-mail list, so I read in your most recent newsletter that you were heading to Mexico with your family. Have fun!"

"Oh wow, thanks," he said, a little stunned. I'd already told him that I read his newsletter and was on his e-mail list at the start of our conversation, but that's easy to say. By mentioning his Mexico trip, I was showing him that I actually read his newsletter. We hung up the phone, and five minutes later I got an e-mail from him that said, "Hey, Stu, I love how you went the extra mile to create content specifically for my audience, and I love that you're part of my community. Send me what I need to promote your seminar."

Obviously, every no won't automatically turn into a yes, but if you stay cool, it keeps the doors open for future partnerships, a relationship, and possibly a lasting friendship. If you're too pushy or get upset, it'll turn people off. So like Fonzie on *Happy Days*, we're all gonna be cool, right?

Also, no matter who says yes and allows you access to their audience, be grateful. Any kind of opportunity you have to be in front of someone else's audience, whether it's a podcast, Facebook live, TikTok, or whatever, is a gift. It's a chance to potentially reach hundreds (or thousands!) of your ideal customers that someone else has spent time and intention finding and building trust with. Don't take that for granted.

Lastly, this strategy only works if you are consistent. This isn't something you can just do once and forget about. This should be a regular part of your marketing rhythm. You always want to be proactively developing and nurturing relationships.

Okay, with all of that in mind, let's get into the "how." For four years, I ran a successful affiliate management company. A big part of my job was researching to find potential affiliates and then reaching out to see if they would be open to some type of collaboration or promotion. Then a consulting client of mine took this process further and simplified it (nicely done, Bryan Harris!). Essentially this outreach process involves four parts: connect, identify the gap, solve the problem, and ask. I'll explain it all using the example of Amy's Airbnb again.

When Amy was looking to build an audience around short-term luxury Airbnb rentals, we found a Facebook group called Short Term University. It was a whole group of people just like Amy, looking to share their tips about managing their properties. That's where she found all the questions about linens, by the way. Amy opened a conversation with the founder of the group by sending this message:

> Hey [name], thank you for the Short Term University Facebook Group. I've been part of it for just over a year. And it has been super helpful. In fact, I got a really good tip from someone in the group regarding software to use for waivers that instantly saved me hours of frustration.
>
> I'm reaching out because I noticed a question that keeps coming up about bed sheets and linens. For example, here are three examples posted in our community.

I share this because one of the things I value with my own short-term rentals is creating magical guest experiences. It's helped me charge three times the normal nightly rate and consistently get rebookings. And one of the keys to that has been sourcing high quality towels, bed sheets, and all kinds of little touches that don't cost a lot but make a huge difference for the guests. For example, here is part of a recent review from one of our guests. This guest immediately rebooked for next year and referred three other guests who all booked for four-plus nights.

There are plenty of throws/blankets and linens for everyone. Honestly, Amy provides a no-expense-was-spared feeling. For me, this trip was equivalent to a warm personal version of the Four Season Hotel private lake house experience.

So if you'd like, **I'd be happy to share my Top 10 Little Touches** that get guests leaving five stars and rebooking. We could share this as a Facebook Live in the group. You win because it's a super valuable piece of content that serves your audience that you don't have to prepare, your audience wins because it's going to help them find the high-quality items they're asking for and get rave reviews, and I win because I get to reach a new audience. It's the trifecta. What do you think? Are you interested?

P.S. I can share other lessons around how to create a magical guest experience as well. So if you'd like me to tailor the teaching element, just let me know.

So, what are we doing here in this message? Let's dissect it.

1. **Connect**. This all starts with you just sending a message. An e-mail. A Facebook message. An Instagram direct message. You have to get the conversation started somehow. In the opening sentence of this message, Amy shares that she's been a part of the group for a year

and has gained incredible value from it. And even better, she shares what specifically she gained from the group. By showing that she's a part of the community already, she instantly forms a connection with who she's reaching out to. Now, if someone is on your cold list, even if you haven't been part of their community, find *some* way to connect. Remember the example with David Frey earlier? So comment on a recent podcast episode or social media post, anything to show that you've done some research and know who you're talking to—and be *specific*!

2. **Identify the gap**. After you've made a connection, you want to show them that their audience is struggling with some kind of knowledge gap. This works best if you can find actual examples of people in their community asking a question. But it doesn't have to be comments in a group. It could be questions on a blog post, comments on social media, ideas people have tweeted, questions left on YouTube videos, etc. And since you have a crossover audience (and you've done all of that amazing Messaging Map research!), you probably already know a lot of the problems their people face. Identify which problems you can best solve and share proof of that.
3. **Solve the problem**. Next you need to suggest a way you can help this person solve the problem and therefore help their audience by closing the gap. Amy proves that she has already solved the problem of where to get bedsheets and linens, and moreover how to provide a no-expenses-spared experience that guests love with little low-cost touches. Amy shows that her methods have already resulted in what every Airbnb host wants: five-star reviews and rebookings. Then she suggests working together and provides a couple of simple ideas, making for an easy yes.
4. **Ask**. Don't overcomplicate this one. Just ask and let it be. Don't hem and haw or offer any disclaimers. Don't give them too much information. Amy says

simply, "What do you think? Are you interested?" And leaves it at that. All you want at this point is a "yes, I'm interested." From there you can sort out the details.

5. **Bonus P.S.** Amy added the P.S. in her message to feel out if there was something else they'd like her to present on. A P.S. offers flexibility and lets people know you're open to feedback if they'd rather you teach something else.

Remember, you are doing these people a favor. They want to serve their audience. And if there are questions that keep popping up that aren't getting addressed, then you are doing them a service by giving them the ability to solve a problem for their audience in a way that doesn't cost them anything. Also, chances are, these creators are on the hook themselves to create content. So you're saving them time by creating something valuable that they don't have to. It's a win for their audience and it's a win for them as a creator.

Of course, plenty of people will say no, and plenty more might not even respond. But remember, it has nothing to do with you! People are busy and have a million other things going on. But all it takes is one yes and you're instantly now in front of an audience you didn't have before. I guarantee if you use this strategy and stick with it, you *will* get to a yes. And that yes will lead you to the next yes and the one after that! Then, when you get a yes, just deliver an awesome lesson with the five-part framework you already learned.

There are plenty of other creators out there who would love to have you share with their audience. Make borrowing some influence a regular part of your marketing rhythm, and it will grow your audience, your list, your business, and help you build incredible relationships along the way. Because, just between us, building a business is *hard*. It can feel like no one else in your life is doing what you're doing. You don't have to go it alone. Find your community and help each other out!

CHAPTER 16

THE FASTEST AND EASIEST WAY TO LAUNCH YOUR MEMBERSHIP

What if I told you it's time to launch? *But Stu, I don't even have a membership yet! I don't have content or a website or a sales page!* Guess what? You don't need any of that to make some money right now and build momentum for your membership.

It's time to dive into what I call the founding member launch—a strategy that will not only get you out of your own way but will jumpstart your membership. It's basically this: **you put out an invitation for others to join your membership right now, before it even exists, and then you let them help you create it.** In fact, this book and my flagship course, The Membership Experience, wouldn't even exist if it hadn't been for a founding member launch.

Normally, people get stuck overthinking, overanalyzing, and waiting for the "perfect time." And because of that, they don't move forward with their ideas. But this process is so stinkin' simple that you could actually launch your membership within an hour.

Resist the negative thoughts of "I don't have any content yet" or "I should wait until my audience is bigger" or "the timing is off" or "I need to learn more before I launch." Those are what we call the "gremlins." Instead, embrace the idea that it *is* possible. Thousands of people in our community have already done it! You can do this too if you keep moving forward. Embrace the fact that the process can be simple. The simplicity is what makes it so special. It eliminates excuses. It forces you to just take the next step—and that's the key to getting going.

Here's how it works . . .

STEP 1: SHARE YOUR IDEA

You begin by simply writing a blog post, Facebook post, or social media post. Heck, you could also do this with a YouTube video, podcast episode, or Instagram reel. But here's the key: you're going to make this post wherever you are currently communicating with your audience. So if your people are on LinkedIn, then you will make this post there. If they're on Facebook, do it there. Wherever you have an audience of 200-plus people, that's where you're going to make this post. Make sense? And if you don't have an audience of 200-plus yet, no problem. That's what the previous chapters were for. You'll have an audience to launch to in no time flat if you follow what we've outlined.

Once you've picked the platform you're going to make the announcement on, what do you actually say? The first part of the message is going to focus solely on the idea. What is it and where did it come from? You want to share the moment that sparked the idea.

Maybe you belong to another membership and it triggered a thought that you could do something similar for your market. Or perhaps you were watching a video where this very enthusiastic Canadian was talking about a membership site and you thought, *this would be an incredible way to serve and support my audience*. Wherever the idea came from, your first step is to explain it, trace its roots, and set the stage for something big.

The best part is, when you're sharing this message, you don't have to create anything "fancy" like a sales page, webinar, or ad campaign. Whether it's through an e-mail, a Facebook post, or an Instagram video, the goal is to plant that seed of curiosity in your audience's mind. You might say, "It got me thinking about you and how valuable it would be to have a place where people like us, working toward [ABC outcome] could gather, get the support we need, and make massive progress together." Don't worry if you feel like you're still figuring it all out—that's the magic of the founding member launch. It's about transparency, not perfection.

In fact, sharing that this idea is raw and you don't have everything figured out yet helps explain one of the *big* benefits of becoming a founding member—a discounted price (which we'll talk about in a minute).

STEP 2: CAST THE VISION

Now, you shift gears. You're not unveiling a polished masterpiece; you're just casting a vision, painting a picture of what this idea could become. You could share something like, "While it's just an idea now, here's what I envision it transforming into . . . " This step is where you articulate the potential of your brainchild. It's your opportunity to make your audience see what you see, feel what you feel, and become a part of something greater. The beauty here is that you're not promising a finished product; you're inviting them to be a part of shaping it.

Nicholas Wilton, my friend who joined my IMPACT mastermind, runs a membership and multimillion-dollar business called Art2Life, where he teaches people how to level up their art and create a successful career doing it. But before he did any of that, he shared his idea with a group of people who were taking his course. He explained, "I've been thinking about creating a community where we can continue this experience, not just for 12 weeks, but all year long. I envision it becoming a place where . . ." And just like that, he cast the vision for his membership.

To see Nicholas Wilton's full case study, head to predictableprofitsbook.com.

Nicholas initially shared this with roughly 200 people, and over 180 of them signed up for a monthly membership at $30 per month. That's over $5,400 per month in recurring revenue *before* the membership had been fully created!

STEP 3: MAKE AN INVITATION

With the groundwork laid, it's time for the main event: the invitation. You extend a warm invitation to your audience, encouraging them to join you as founding members. You might say, "I don't know if this idea resonates with you, but if it does, I want you to be a part of this journey from the very beginning." You're offering them the chance to help mold the direction of your membership, becoming pioneers alongside you. And of course, they get the perk of a founding member price that will stay that low forever, even when you raise the price for your membership down the line. As long as they stay a member in good standing, this is a big incentive for people to join because those ongoing savings really start to add up.

This could look like, "I invite you to become a founding member. One of the big benefits of joining now is that you get in at the lowest price this is ever going to be. And you'll be locked in at this price for as long as you stay a member in good standing. *Plus* I want you to contribute feedback and ideas to make this the best place for all of us on our journey toward [DESIRED OUTCOME]. You'll have a direct hand in shaping the membership as it grows by giving your ideas and insights as this is being built."

Jen Waldman did this not long ago. She is the founder and director of a training center for Broadway actors. Jen uses her experience in acting, storytelling, and communication to help other leaders and companies build a culture of creativity. After running her brick-and-mortar studio for 19 years, she decided to start a membership to help more people and allow her more flexibility in her own life. So she did a founding member launch.

She didn't run ads, webinars, or even post on social media. All she did was send out one-to-one personalized e-mails. She sent 138 e-mails and welcomed 69 people who joined at the introductory price of $79 per month! That's $5,451 worth of recurring revenue right out of the gate by only sending e-mails! Jen did a "real" launch a few months later, upped the price to $99, and welcomed in many more members—proof that if you just make a genuine, enticing invitation, you never know what will happen.

STEP 4: GIVE A CLEAR CALL TO ACTION

Here comes the pivot: your call to action. It's straightforward and critical. Guide your audience on what to do next. You might ask them to send you a direct message, click a link, or leave a comment. My favorite is to ask people to send me a direct message because that way my fragile ego stays protected whether one person or one hundred are interested. This step is all about simplicity and clarity. By making it easy for people to take that next step, you're paving the way for their journey as founding members. This is where you might get nervous because now is where things get real. You're finally making an ask! That's why the least scary thing to do is to ask people to send you a direct message if they're interested.

Just find five seconds of courage and hit "post." Remember, you can do this.

STEP 5: FOLLOW UP

The final stride is the follow-up. When you get those enthusiastic direct messages or comments, it's time to seal the deal. Provide people with the link to join as founding members, whether it's a checkout page or a simple PayPal link. Don't get caught up thinking you have to overcomplicate it. Keep it simple. This is the point at which your vision transforms into reality. And guess what? You just started a membership!

Let me tell you about one of my favorite membership students, Anna Saucier. Years ago, Anna and her husband struggled to get pregnant. Her journey through infertility and the uphill climb to parenthood gave her a deep understanding of infertility as a symptom of other underlying health issues. She was passionate about helping other women like her, so she became an infertility practitioner and saw one-on-one clients.

But after she gave birth to her two kids, Anna struggled to find time for her clients, while also finding herself answering the same questions over and over again. That's when she decided to start a membership, to serve more people and create time freedom. Anna had no name recognition or social media presence. She had a small Facebook group of 326 people. She didn't have a website for her membership, a name, or much of a plan yet at all. But she had desire and gumption. So she decided to do a founding member launch. Here are some bits from her original post:

> *Can I share something a little personal with you?*
>
> *I LOVE helping FCPs and other NFP/FABM instructors grow profitable businesses. It's been my passion for quite a while now. I've dabbled in a few different ways to help, but I know now that the best way to help them is on an ongoing basis, month after month.*
>
> *So I'm planning on launching a membership site that does exactly that . . .*
>
> *It's not cheap. In fact, it's several thousand dollars. But that's how strong my commitment is to helping instructors grow profitable businesses . . .*
>
> *I'm opening up a limited number of lifetime spots when it opens up for just $249. . . . But here's the catch. I'm only offering this for 24 hours . . .*
>
> *So if you'd like to join me in this, send me a message by Monday (tomorrow) at 3 P.M., and I'll send you details on how to make your payment.*
>
> *Peace,*
> *Anna*

As you can see, Anna's membership is pricey. It might be much more than yours will be. And yet, in just 24 hours, she closed her founding member launch with 17 members and $4,233 in revenue. A few months later, after refining the process and material with her founding members, she launched again and gained 34 new people, bringing her membership total to 56. It was life-changing for her business, confidence, and family.

Here are a few quick tips to consider when you implement the founding member launch for yourself:

1. **Embrace the emotions.** You might be scared. That's okay! That's normal! Almost everyone is. Summon the courage and go for it.
2. **Don't overthink this.** Lean in to the simplicity. This is nothing more than a test.
3. **Put it on the calendar.** Write it down. Make a date with yourself and make it happen.
4. **Keep the launch brief.** Don't keep the offer open for more than a few days.
5. **Communicate often with your audience.** Post about it a few times. Remind everyone that the offer expires.
6. **When it comes to pricing, lean toward a low-price, no-brainer offer.** We're going for an easy yes here. While the money is great, it's not the main goal. Getting some momentum and creating wins for your customers is. You'll also want room to raise the price after you've created and tested the content. So when in doubt, go low.
7. **Manage the expectations of your customers.** The tech won't be great. There will be glitches. This is the first iteration and it will only get better. Be transparent about this.
8. **Manage your expectations.** There will be bumps. It'll be okay. Stay humble, learn from them, and keep going.

9. **Connect and collaborate.** Double down on serving your clients. Serve the heck out of them. Treat them like the most important people in the world. Help them get some amazing results and welcome their feedback. This is all a chance for you to learn as much as you can and create the best membership in the future.

Lastly, and most importantly, what we really want here is to create great results for your customers. That's the biggest win. We're looking for success stories. *I made my first sale! I played my first song! I've tried everything and this is the first time I've ever made progress! I wrote my first chapters! I gained so much clarity! I had the hard conversation!* Etc., etc., etc. You want to help your clients make progress in some meaningful way, both for your own confidence and for theirs. These stories will be the best testament to the power of your membership. And here are a few more benefits of the Founding Member Launch.

1. It creates idea validation and confidence for you.

Imagine validating your idea before investing countless hours in creating it. By gauging real interest through founding member commitments, you ensure that your efforts are focused on something your audience really wants. Plus, you're generating revenue upfront—and being paid to build something is a concept that's exciting in itself.

Your confidence will grow as you witness the momentum of your founding member launch. With every commitment, you'll be propelled forward, knowing that your idea resonates. This confidence becomes the wind beneath your wings as you move toward launching to the general public, setting the stage for an impactful membership experience. And worst-case scenario: if nobody takes you up on your offer, no harm, no foul. You haven't wasted a ton of time building a product, and you don't have to face public rejection. Plus, you've learned something tremendously valuable: what you wanted to offer is out of alignment with what your audience wants. It's better to learn that before spending time, energy, and money creating it, right?

2. It's an early advantage for your founding members.

Your founding members reap the rewards of their commitment. They secure a coveted spot on the ground floor, a place of privilege. The founding member price is not just a number; it's a symbol of their foresight, a constant reminder that they were the pioneers who believed in your vision from the outset. But they gain more than a price advantage, they gain influence. They shape the trajectory of your membership by providing feedback and insights as you fine-tune the experience. This level of involvement fosters a sense of ownership and camaraderie that lasts beyond the launch as you co-create your membership together.

3. It helps you overcome your hesitations.

Of course, hesitation can creep in—the fear of imperfection, the worry that nobody will buy, and the apprehension of putting yourself out there. The founding member launch is designed to dismantle these barriers. The beauty is in the simplicity. Remember our philosophy: don't overcomplicate things. The simpler, the better. It's not about perfection; it's about progress. By taking action and embracing imperfection, you're moving forward and creating momentum and accountability for yourself.

The founding member launch is an experiment, a learning experience. If nobody joins, it's not a failure; it's a valuable lesson. You'll gain insights into your messaging, allowing you to refine and adapt. Remember that you're not looking for just interest; you're looking for actual commitment, and that's a different ball game. When people pull out their wallets and (digitally) hand over their hard-earned cash, now you really have something. You have a validated idea, a commitment to ensure you follow through, and people to help you do it.

Listen, this approach works so brilliantly not because it's magic, but because it's psychology. It's about harnessing the power of momentum, and the founding member launch is your means for doing so. It's also about more than just a launch; it's about cultivating a community, fostering connection, and embarking on a shared adventure.

So go ahead, take the leap, embrace imperfection, and let your founding member launch be the kick in the pants you need to get things going.

As we move forward, the question becomes, *How* do I deliver content that gets my audience incredible results? Specifically, how do you do this within your membership? Well, buckle up, my friend. We're about to talk about all things content.

ACTION STEPS

1. Decide what you stand for. Write out your list of values and do some deep thinking about your "why."
2. Pick your platform! Simple as that.
3. Create at least a month's worth of platform content using the 10 x 3 Framework. Come up with 10 problems and 3 solutions to those problems for your market.
4. Make your list-builder. You can choose whichever you'd like, but I recommend the curated PDF or answer guide.
5. Set up your landing page. Remember, the most important thing is the headline. Nail that and you're in good shape.
6. Borrow some influence by reaching out to those who already have a platform and offering to be of service.
7. Do a founding member launch! I'm serious, do it. Before you move on, I challenge you to fire off a message and get people to commit right now. You can do it!

CREATING TOGETHER IS BETTER

PART III

SERVE YOUR PEOPLE

Now that you have an audience of people who are interested in your topic and see you as a go-to expert, it's time to create the content for your membership. And, if you've done a founding member launch, you already have members! So you better get cracking on what you're going to put inside. In Part III, I'll teach you how to plan, structure, and create the content of your membership. Your goal is always to provide valuable information that helps your members achieve a transformation—but that content should be easy for you to create and maintain. We will also explore how to craft content that facilitates progress and generates the Circle of Awesomeness™.

But first I want you to remember this: you're likely not the only one who has ever taught this topic. And it's at this point that I see people's gremlins creep in again. They start doubting themselves or their ability to teach. "Who am I to share this info?" or "Why would anyone listen to me? I don't have any fancy degrees."

You might not have any letters after your name or any formal education on the topic, but you have the most valuable thing of all:

a result that your audience wants to replicate or obtain. You know something they want to know or have done something they want to do. *And* since you've now started your own Circle of Awesomeness, you've helped a few others with this too. So as you go through this section, ask yourself, *How could this be applied to my market or my business?* If you do that, it will open your brain to finding exactly what you need to create an *amazing* experience for your members while minimizing the time and effort you need to deliver that experience. You ready? Let's go!

CHAPTER 17

THE FOUR DIFFERENT MEMBERSHIP MODELS

There are four different types of membership models you could create—four different ways you could serve your people. As we discuss these models, I want you to think about how you see them in action in everyday life all around you and work through which model makes the most sense for your business.

First up, **knowledge-based memberships** teach people a skill, help them solve an ongoing problem, or make something more convenient in their lives. There's a good chance you have some kind of amazing knowledge in your head that other people will pay for. Can you teach people to master an ability? Do people regularly ask you the same questions over and over? Are you the go-to person in your community around a subject? Maybe you even have a professional expertise that you can turn into a recurring model from a one-on-one business.

This type of membership delivers content through videos, audios, and text. It's technologically simple to implement because it's all based online, accessible anywhere. My membership falls into this category. I have a membership for people who have memberships (meta, I know!). The majority of my students also fall into this category. Like Susan Garrett, who teaches people how to train their dogs; Joy Anderson, who helps people grow preschools; or Levi Kujala, who has a membership teaching others to play the guitar.

The value of knowledge-based memberships is *not* in how much information you offer your customers but the speed at which they can implement what you're sharing—and ultimately, the speed at which they can see some kind of progress in their life.

To see full case studies with Susan Garrett and Levi Kujala, head to predictableprofitsbook.com.

It's so easy to fall into the trap of thinking that the more content you give, the more value you create. But that's not true. In fact, loading people up with a ton of information will overwhelm your members *and* it will burn you out as well. So one of the keys to a knowledge-based membership is to obsess over the progress of your members. (File that one away—we'll come back to it later.)

For now, let's explore some quick examples. Novella A. Prempeh is a good one. She runs a knowledge-based membership in the UK that teaches parents how to confidently care for their children's natural hair—especially really curly hair or hair that is difficult to grow. In fact, I personally picked up a number of tips from her when it came to caring for my son's hair. In her case, she's teaching parents how to identify what hair type their child has, the best way to care for it, and how to create a regimen that works to maximize growth.

> ***One of the keys to a knowledge-based membership is to obsess over the progress of your members.***

My student Lisa K., who I mentioned earlier, runs a membership that teaches people how to make better decisions using their intuition. If you've never used your intuition to make decisions before, you're probably not even aware that it's happening. Lisa teaches students how to better tune in to that inner knowing that is guiding them. Developing this skill takes time—and that's why it works well for a knowledge-based membership.

Lastly, Julie Soul started a business right in the middle of the pandemic. She launched a membership called Soul Sparklettes. Instead of parents having to come up with their own ideas to entertain their bored kids, Julie delivers monthly art projects that can be done at home.

Many of the other examples I've used throughout this book like art, relationships, weight loss, and mastering Microsoft Excel are all knowledge-based memberships as well because they are the easiest and quickest to start.

But while the primary focus of this book is knowledge-based memberships, the lessons in it apply to every model. If you plan to create one of the other three types, don't count yourself out. Continuously ask: *How can I apply this to my membership?* Plus I'll give you bonus information along the way for tips and tricks that apply to each kind of membership. Never look for how this *won't* work. Instead, examine how it *will* and how you can use the same principles.

Next up is the **product-based membership** model, where members receive a product each month. Think of popular companies like Dollar Shave Club. Remember when you actually had to go buy razors at the drug store? I remember being so annoyed (and weirdly embarrassed) when I had to go find an employee and be like, "Can you please open this locked case? I need a razor." But not anymore. Razors come straight to our door.

BarkBox, Birchbox, and other subscription boxes are other examples of this model. My friend Sarah Williams has a subscription box membership. Her boxes are full of personalized shirts, monogrammed bags, cups, and jewelry for women. Every month she gets tons of e-mails from customers expressing how excited they are when they see those blue boxes on their doorstep. It's like someone picked out a present just for them. A few years after launching her subscription box, she also launched a second membership (because she was receiving so many questions from people on how to do that). So her second membership (knowledge-based) coaches other subscription box owners who send monthly gifts to everyone from dentists to planner-lovers to crafters to even one specifically for guinea pig enthusiasts. She shares all about this process in her book, *One Box At a Time*.

To see Sarah Williams's full case study, head to predictableprofitsbook.com.

The third model is a **service-based membership** where members pay a monthly fee for a certain number of services. An example is Mary-Claire Fredette's massage membership. This is a common model for brick-and-mortar stores, as well as any provider who wants to work on a retainer.

Take, for example, the car wash across from my office. One single car wash is $10, but their membership for unlimited car washes is $12 per month. If you get your car washed twice a month, you've already gotten a great deal! As someone who loves a clean car, I was all over this. I joined that membership so fast and basically get my car washed every time I'm at the office. I asked the employee the last time I was there how many people have joined their membership so far, and he said 4,500!

Think about that for a second. That car wash owner knows with certainty that 4,500 customers will be paying them at the beginning of the month. Now, don't you think that car wash is enjoying much higher profits and much lower stress than the one down the road who just hopes customers come by each month when they decide their car is dirty? Anyone who offers a service that is often viewed as a one-time transaction—like a haircut, massage, or car wash—can use this model to create recurring monthly revenue.

The fourth type is a **community-based membership**, where members pay to belong to a group with shared interests. This model provides access to a community of like-minded individuals. This includes groups and platforms where the main benefit offered is the ability to connect with others who share your enthusiasm about a topic.

Years ago, I bought my first car. It was a Mini Cooper, and it was amazing. I'll never forget that shortly after that, I got a call from our Mini dealership and they asked, "Hey, do you want to come join us for a Mini rally?" It was one of the easiest yeses of my life. As Mini owners, we all got together and parked in a massive outdoor movie theater to watch *The Italian Job*. I'll never forget the scene where Charlize Theron speeds on-screen in her red Mini Cooper and we all honked our horns together and cheered. It was incredible.

What made it so magical was that there was something we all understood: the magic of the Mini. Everybody there was a Mini enthusiast. And if you don't get it, well, that's just fine. That membership's not for you. Your membership doesn't have to be based on teaching or offering services. It can simply be about bringing people who have a shared interest together.

In Estonia, Tanel Jappinen has a community-based membership for parents who want to connect on the joys and hardships of parenting, and how to do it better. He doesn't consider himself a parenting expert; he just wants to be intentional about the way he raises his kids and wants to connect with others who want to do the same.

So which one resonates most with you? A knowledge, product, service, or community-based membership? Also know that your membership can be any combination of them! Many knowledge-based memberships have a community element. People who are interested in learning something are often interested in connecting with others who are learning too. Decide what model you want to commit to now and let's keep going.

CHAPTER 18

KNOWLEDGE-BASED MEMBERSHIPS

Since knowledge-based membership models are the most common type, we're going to dive into them here. (But if you're thinking of a product, service, or community-based membership, don't tune out! There's something for you to learn here as well!) There are five different content models to consider for knowledge-based memberships. Let's decide which one is right for you. There are pros and cons to each, and they're all just a personal choice—there's no better or worse model.

As we unpack these, I want you to pay attention to your reactions. If one of them resonates with you, make a note of it. By the end of this chapter, I want you to have an idea of what your content model will be. Once you're clear on that, it'll be much easier for you to create the content that goes inside.

First up is the **publisher model**. Think of this like an online magazine. Each month, you're producing new content that goes into the membership. But keep in mind, you're not just producing a ton of content. You want to limit it to four primary pieces of content per month, meaning one primary piece of content per week. People don't have a lot of excess time to constantly consume content. We also need to create space for people to implement what they're learning. So, one primary piece of content per week is a great rhythm to maintain that balance. And we want each of piece of content to be no more than 60 to 90 minutes, otherwise you'll lose people and they'll feel overwhelmed. Though, for the record, they don't have to be 60 to 90 minutes. They can often be much shorter. It's really about delivering the right amount of content to equip your audience to take action.

A great example of this is my student Mim Jenkinson. She runs a membership called the Secret Sticker Society, where she teaches students how to make stickers. Thinking back to our Messaging Map, Mim isn't just helping people learn how to create stickers, she's opening up with creativity, helping them find joy, and even helping them create income for their family. Each week she publishes new instructions, templates, trainings, and examples for her community.

Next up is the **UPS model**. This is like delivering a package of content each month. A great example of this is the TeenLife Ministries membership that was run by Paul Evans. (He has since sold it.) He provided pre-done sermons that youth ministers could use to mix with their own messages. It saved them so much time and energy, which is important because many youth pastors also have other jobs, so they're always strapped for time! Note that Paul isn't actually teaching anything. He's not helping them get better or providing speaking tips. He's just delivering sermons they can tailor and make their own. And because he is eliminating so much of the work for overwhelmed youth pastors like him, they can spend more time with their families and focus on the needs of their students. That's where the value comes from—saving them the time and stress of staying up late every Saturday night, trying to prepare their sermons last minute.

The third model is the **coaching model**. This one is more hands-on. It might involve group coaching, masterminds, or accountability elements. It's about coaching people through the process and helping them experience progress. My good friend Amy Porterfield's Momentum Membership is a great example here. It's a community for her Digital Course Academy alumni. If you've been through her course and want more support around creating, launching, or scaling your course business, you can sign up to get coached more intimately by Amy and her team.

I have a similar model for alumni of The Membership Experience. Though to use the coaching model, you certainly don't have to only use it on the back end of a course. Sharon Pope is a relationship coach and has a membership where she coaches women who are contemplating a divorce. Making that decision is incredibly hard, and many women feel paralyzed. Sharon coaches them through how to make the decision to either fix their marriage or move forward without regret.

The next model is the **drip, or modular, model**. This is where you drip out content over a set amount of time. When Yuri Elkaim, a holistic nutritionist, started his membership to help other healthpreneurs start their businesses, he created a curriculum that lasts over three years. When someone joins his membership, they get content every single day for three years. It's all delivered in bite-sized chunks.

It's dripped out similar to a course. Members don't get access all at once, and to get the rest of the material, you have to stay subscribed. But Yuri didn't start his membership with this much content. He started with just a few months' worth, and it grew from there.

The final model is the **combo model**. This is just what it sounds like. It pulls different elements from all of the models. It might include multiple models in one, like a publisher format with a coaching component. Scott Paley and Joan Garry's Nonprofit Leadership Lab does this well. They publish new information each week and also include time-saving resources and templates. Joan also provides seminars that serve as consulting and coaching sessions, something that would be wildly expensive and way out of the budget for most nonprofits if they were looking for one-on-one time. And bonus, they also have a community where nonprofit leaders can support each other.

It's common for memberships to have a community component, because even when a community-based membership is not the main offering, members often want to chat with each other. Susan Bradley also runs a combination model. She serves e-commerce owners and each month provides content, but she also has coaches within her membership who specialize in different areas. Throughout the month, these coaches are available to answer questions and provide feedback. If they want additional one-on-one help, they can purchase extra sessions inside the membership. Susan, too, has a community component where the members can chat with each other and discuss the different ideas that are being shared.

Now, I want you to pick a model that you feel is going to best serve your members and feels most natural to how you want to operate. Would it be a publisher, UPS, coaching, drip, or combo model? If committing to creating new content every single week feels scary to you, don't do that! If you don't want to provide support through coaching, you don't have to. You want to serve your members well, but never forget that this is also supposed to be fun and help create the life you want to live. Don't worry if you're not sure exactly what content you're going to create yet. The clarity will come as you start moving forward. So make a decision and start putting one foot in front of the other.

CHAPTER 19

THE #1 REASON PEOPLE CANCEL . . . AND HOW TO PREVENT IT

One of the biggest objections I hear to starting a membership is: But what if people cancel? I'm going to tell you right here and right now the number one reason people cancel so you can avoid it from the get-go. And it's not what you might think, though it is the same reason no matter what industry you're in or what model you choose.

The number one reason people cancel is . . . overwhelm. Basically: *too much content.*

Yup, that's right, you are going to want to provide much less content than you probably think. Overwhelm happens when members can't keep up with the volume of content you're providing. This plants a seed of doubt in their minds, making them question whether they can ever achieve the results they're after. We want wins, not doubts! If that seed of doubt is planted, it's only a matter of time before they cancel. If your people are paying for products or services each month that they never use and they watch them just stack up, they'll cancel. Less is more. This even happens with product or service memberships.

So what's the solution? It's simple, but it's also counterintuitive. **The value of a membership doesn't come from the volume of content you provide. Instead, it comes from the speed at which people can implement the information you provide.**

Again, it's not about volume; it's about speed of implementation. Think about this for yourself right now. You're reading this book because you want to launch a profitable membership. If you had the choice of going through 10 hours of content or 3 hours while still getting the same result, what would you choose?

So it's not about the volume of content. It's always about the speed at which people can get to a result.

This is good news for us! It means we don't have to create a ton of content. I know some people love to create content. Maybe you even *want* to create a lot. Regardless, it's natural to think that the more you provide, the more value you create. But when it comes to memberships, it's just not true. Instead, focus on creating content that moves people forward in the fastest way possible. If you can get someone a result in 3 steps instead of 10, always go with 3. Once again, the value you provide does not depend on how much content you provide, but how quickly people can get results.

I first discovered the true power of the bite-sized content when I was reading the book *ReWork*, by Jason Fried and David Heinemeier Hansson. Most business books have chapters that are 20 to 30 pages long. So my usual struggle is that I attempt to do my reading before going to bed, and inevitably, I fall asleep before finishing the chapter (doh!) and end up reading the same darn chapter over and over again later. Obviously, this isn't going to work if you want to make any meaningful progress through the book.

> ***The value you provide does not depend on how much content you provide, but how quickly people can get results.***

But with *ReWork*, the experience was *much* different. The chapters in that book are very short. Sometimes just a page or two. So instead of feeling defeated because I wasn't completing any chapters, I was making real progress. And before I knew it, one chapter led to two. Two led to five. And because I now had momentum on my side, I kept going. Without even realizing it, I had polished off more than 10 chapters. Think about the difference that feeling produces. Before I was defeated, but now I was fired up and telling everybody about that book. Heck, over a decade later, I'm still talking about it.

Isn't that what we want for our members? The "experience" of what we provide—the sense of accomplishment and momentum—is *so* important. Because if we deliver content in a way that puts people to sleep, we don't end up serving anyone.

Let's look at some examples. Remember Paul Evans, who ran the ministry membership site? He used to pack endless stuff into his membership. Lessons, a community element, PowerPoint presentations, templates, etc. His business was doing okay, but he was having trouble growing. So much so that he was even considering closing it down. But first he surveyed his members and asked them: "If we were to get rid of everything inside the membership, what's the number one thing you would want us to keep?"

The overwhelming response to Paul's question was the PowerPoint presentations. Youth pastors found it so time-consuming and tedious to put together their own sermons that it was pretty much all they wanted from Paul. So Paul cut out everything else, saving himself about 75 percent of the workload, and focused the membership on the one thing his members valued the most. As a result, he created a better experience for his members, all while eliminating a ton of work for himself.

Suzi Dafnis runs a membership called HerBusiness over in Australia. It's a supportive and collaborative network for women entrepreneurs looking to grow and scale. After surveying her members, she found out they weren't looking for more information.

Instead, they were looking for more accountability. So without having to create a bunch of new content, Suzi reimagined her membership experience to provide just that by creating a process to pair up members to hold each other accountable.

The thing that people really want from you—the thing they most value and find most helpful—might not be what you think it is. At the beginning of your membership, you might not know exactly what this is yet, and that's okay. Do a founders' launch, decide on your content model, and start creating membership content. After you have a few customers, ask them about what they love most. This will keep you focused on what really moves the needle, instead of needlessly creating lots more content that they don't even want!

Say it with me one more time: **the key to a successful membership site isn't about providing a ton of content. It's about helping your members implement what they learn as quickly as possible.** "Quick wins" is the name of the game! Keep this in mind as we move forward and dig into what to provide inside your membership.

MODULE V
TO DO
BLOG
TO DO
MODULE VI
MODULE VIII
BLOG
TO DO
BLOG

CHAPTER 20

YOUR SUCCESS PATH: A BLUEPRINT FOR YOU AND YOUR MEMBERS

There is one secret (well, not anymore!) little tool that's going to help you differentiate your membership from everything else in the market and lead to never-ending success. It's called a Success Path™, and yes, it lives up to its name.

Let's break it down. A Success Path starts with where your members are now and ends with where they want to be. This is similar to the Messaging Map, but now instead of two stages (their "now" and their "future"), you're going to clearly communicate the journey in its entirety. Imagine a starting point and a final outcome. Like somebody going from never having picked up a guitar to playing on huge stages, like the next Eric Clapton. Or never having picked up a paintbrush to becoming the next Picasso. Going from a messed-up marriage to one that is thriving and happy. In each of these examples, somebody is not going to instantly go from their starting point to the final outcome, right? There is a progression.

Think of the Success Path like a playbook. With a Success Path, you're walking people through the specific things they need to master at each stage of their journey. Step by step, stage by stage, you are ultimately leading them to the final outcome they're after.

But here's the secret to all of this: every moment of progress equals a moment of success. And as long as somebody is experiencing some kind of success, they're never going to leave.

> ***Every moment of progress equals a moment of success.***

In all the years I've been doing this, I've never known anybody to leave a membership because they've experienced too much success. The Success Path is how you help your members to *keep* experiencing success all along their membership journey. In short, the Success Path is everything! And it affects:

1. Your content
2. Your marketing
3. Your member retention

Here's the power of it. Brenda Ster had run a social marketing coaching business for years and had just established a membership built primarily on word of mouth that served over 3,000 people in its first year. But she lost nearly 50 percent of her members when it came time for them to renew the following year.

To try to improve her member retention (and hopefully attract new members), she ramped up her content creation into overdrive. She went live in her group multiple times a week and created more printables, workbooks, templates, videos, and trainings. *More value!* she thought, but really, she was creating more overwhelm. And as you now know, that's not good!

Through TME, she completely transformed her membership. The first thing she did was create a Success Path so members knew exactly where they were headed. She also cut down on the content and only included what directly helped her customers move along through each milestone on their Success Path. She relaunched her membership a few months after starting the course and gained 484 new members, resulting in a 6-figure launch.

That's the power of the Success Path. It acts like a magnet for potential members because it breaks what can seem like an overwhelming and complex journey down into the few things that really matter right now. It emphasizes that they don't have to learn everything right now. And that's a *big* stress relief.

The thing I appreciate about Brenda is that she was open to change, even though it meant reorganizing content that she had for years around what was a new concept to her at the time. But the Success Path had a big impact on her membership, so much so that Brenda spoke at The Membership Experience Live conference and talked through how she created it and the difference it made for her business.

If you want to see the whole presentation, head to predictableprofitsbook.com.

In the next few chapters, we're going to break down how to create the Success Path for your members into step-by-step, bite-sized chunks. And in fact, you may be on a Success Path of your own at this very minute!

CHAPTER 21

STAGES AND CHARACTERISTICS

It's time to get into the nitty-gritty details. Let's roll up our sleeves and dive headfirst into building your very own Success Path, starting with the stages and characteristics of your members at each point in the process.

The good news is: you are not starting from scratch. You've already done your Messaging Map (Chapter 5), and that valuable work is about to pay off. You have already laid out two critical points: the present and the desired future. You've already researched and discovered where your audience is now and where they aspire to be. Now we just need to identify the essence of your Success Path by creating clarity about what the journey looks like in between these two points.

Let me reiterate the significance of these two anchor points—you are:

1) Starting with the now

2) Painting a vivid picture of the future

Think about what your audience is thinking, feeling, and doing in both of these states. When you created your Messaging Map, you essentially sketched out these two cornerstones already. Our objective now is to flesh out the phases your members will go through as they progress from their starting to their ending point.

1. *Decide on a beginning stage and ending stage.* We just went over this, but I cannot emphasize enough the importance of clearly setting these cornerstones. You need to be clear on this so your audience will be clear on what they will be getting from your membership and each stage of success.
2. *Map out a timeline and decide the number of stages between these two endpoints.* Think of the big moments that happen as someone starts to progress on this journey from where they are to where they want to be. Since you've probably already walked through this process yourself and/or have already taught others, I want to encourage you to pinpoint where the biggest feelings of success/achievement/relief were. If you were sitting down with someone, what questions would you ask them to identify where they are on their journey? What are their major turning points and transitions?

   You never want fewer than three stages or more than seven. Fewer than three, and it's not a real journey. More than seven, and it feels too overwhelming. The sweet spot is five. And here's the catch: the early stages should be designed to allow people to move through them the fastest.

   Think of it like a martial arts belt system; the first belts are achievable at a faster pace, just like our initial stages. These stages are about sparking momentum and propelling people forward with the quick wins. As they progress, the journey becomes more nuanced. Once they advance to a black belt, the challenges are greater and the timeline is slightly longer. But by then, people are more committed, so they're more likely to stick with it. This balance between rapid advancement and measured progress is key.
3. *Name the stages.* Get creative as you do this, using empowering names that exude progress and transformation. If you name stage 1 "Loserville," no one's going to want to be a part of that stage, right? At each stage, think about what people will be thinking,

feeling, and doing. But don't stress if the right names don't immediately come to mind. You can always resort to the reliable "Stage 1," "Stage 2," and so forth. That's totally fine for now. If you've implemented everything in the book up until now, you are in the "Serve Your People" stage in the Success Path for this book.

4. *Describe the main component/elements/etc. of each stage.* These detailed descriptions are the lifeblood of your Success Path. They act as a compass for your members, guiding them to their right place on the path. We want members to deeply identify with them. Imagine someone reading these descriptions and thinking, "Yes, that's exactly where I am!" Remember, you've already crafted this for the endpoint stages through the Messaging Map, so you have some practice.

   What should they have accomplished by now? What thoughts, feelings, or roadblocks come along with those accomplishments? For you, right here at the "Serve Your People" stage of this book, you might be feeling confident because you've already made such great progress toward creating your membership, but things are becoming real as you have to start delivering results for them. There's some anxiety that comes with that. Maybe you were working on pure adrenaline at the beginning and now the rubber is hitting the road as things get real. If you did a founding members' launch, you're a business owner! That comes with a new identity you're stepping into, which may include some imposter syndrome.

I've provided a variety of Success Path examples with each stage and their characteristics (and milestones and action items, but we'll get to those next) in the online book resources. You can find those at www.predictableprofitsbook.com.

CHAPTER 22

SUCCESS PATH MILESTONES

Now that you have your stages and characteristics, we're going to dig into milestones. These are the stepping stones that your members will cross as they move through the stages of their Success Path. They serve as powerful indicators of progress. Think of milestones as tangible markers of achievement, much like the skills someone would have to demonstrate different levels of mastery.

Let me paint a picture for you. Imagine yourself in a dojo, donning your pristine white belt. Your eyes linger on the vibrant yellow belt that you don't yet have on the wall, a symbol of mastery you aspire to earn. Now, simply attending lessons won't automatically elevate you to that coveted yellow belt status. Even just practicing the punches and kicks won't earn you the belt either. You have to demonstrate an understanding or level of ability. Until you can do that, you keep practicing. In some cases, it can take years to earn the next belt in karate. Progress isn't merely about just showing up; it's about understanding and application. The same is true for your membership site.

A common pitfall I see in memberships is the progression of members without ensuring they truly comprehend the material *and* have actively implemented it. They learn, learn, learn, and never really get tangible results. This mismatch between expectation and outcome can lead to discouragement, and people canceling their membership. Milestones confirm comprehension, mastery, and growth. They make progress measurable and create accountability.

The first characteristic of a great milestone is that a member can confirm they have achieved it with a resounding "yes" or "no" response. Meaning they have either done it, or they haven't. There's no gray area. This clarity gets rid of any ambiguity, prompting your members to face their accomplishments and gaps head-on. For instance, if we rewind to Chapter 14, I might ask you if you created your landing page. That's a milestone within the "Attract Your People" stage of our Success Path, and the answer is either a definitive yes or no. Have you picked a platform? Have you decided what model of membership you're offering? This creates responsibility and a clear road map for action within each stage. If your answer to any of those questions is no, you know exactly what you need to do to make progress, right? And you shouldn't move on to the next stage until you can answer yes. Plus, if you answer yes, I can say, "Great, can I see them?" Do you see how having a black-and-white milestone automatically has accountability built into it?

> ***Milestones confirm comprehension, mastery, and growth.***

In your membership world, milestones enable members to gauge where they are in their journey. Imagine you're guiding them through website creation. A milestone might be acquiring their website's URL. Similarly, crafting a one-year business plan, a debt pay-off plan, or mastering a guitar riff is distinctly measurable—either you've achieved it or you haven't, indicating whether you can move on to the next stage or not.

Resist the temptation to construct vague milestones. A blurry target can be open to interpretation, which we don't want. We want a clear target so your members can know exactly when they've hit the bull's-eye. For example, if I ask if you're fit, your response might be, "I sure am!" But what does that even mean? If I ask you on a scale of 1 to 10, you might give me a number, but that's just your interpretation. But if I ask whether you've reached a specific push-up count, there's no gray area; you can either do it or you can't. It's not wishy-washy and there's no fudging the answer.

A carefully designed Success Path complete with milestones is transformative. It offers a shared language for tracking progress and provides your members with focus. It's a measuring stick that allows us to get clear on where people are within a stage and headed on the larger journey. The early stages should include simpler milestones to create quick wins and foster momentum and enthusiasm. Later stages can include more challenging milestones, capitalizing on members' growing commitment and expertise.

Think about the role milestones have played in this book! Just as you've achieved different milestones (creating your Messaging Map or making a list-builder) and moved through different stages (The Foundation and Attract Your People), your members will do the same thing within your membership. This connectivity of milestones and stages creates an immersive learning experience, culminating in members being really proud of their progress and achieving their goals.

Now is the time for you to write down your milestones. Here are the things to keep in mind:

1. Write your milestones in the form of a yes-or-no question, where a "yes" would indicate the completion of that particular milestone.
2. Each milestone should be a unit on the measuring stick to keep members accountable.
3. Milestones tell members exactly what they need to do to progress to the next stage.

4. Make your milestones crystal clear. If you're not clear, your members won't be able to know what to do or when they have done it.

In the upcoming chapters, you're going to see how these milestones play a big role in developing your content. They indicate exactly what your members need to do to make progress, and thus what you need to teach your members to help them do it. Just as you've experienced firsthand the excitement of completing a milestone, like your founding member launch, your members will too.

CHAPTER 23

ACTION ITEMS

We've reached the final piece of the Success Path! Now that you have your stages and milestones to hit within each stage, we're going to break it down even further with some action items. Action items are those little steps that people have to do in order to achieve each milestone.

So the progression of the elements looks like this:

action steps → milestones → stages → Success Path

Let's explore a real-world example that you might be experiencing right now. If we take a look back at Chapter 6, one of the milestones for your Success Path here is completing your positioning statement, where you can answer if you've done it with a simple yes or no. But I wouldn't expect you to say yes without completing the action items that I provided: the core values exercise, Messaging Map exercise, and positioning statement exercise. The key to a great action item is that it moves someone closer to reaching the next milestone. They provide your members with clarity on what they need to do in order to achieve those milestones. For each milestone, we want to make sure there's a series of action items associated with it. It could be an exercise or a template to fill out, but it needs to be something to complete that will help you reach that milestone.

Sometimes milestones are big, like "implement a founding member launch" within Stage 2: Attract Your People. But we don't just check that off the list in one go. There are a series of steps that lead to that milestone. That's what we want to get clear about here.

In Chapter 16 I listed out the action items for that milestone. Do you remember what they are? (And more importantly, did you do them?) Here they are again:

1. Share your idea
2. Cast the vision
3. Make an invitation
4. Give a clear call to action
5. Follow up

Your action item for this chapter is to complete writing all your action items for your membership's Success Path. Keep in mind that a Success Path is a living, breathing document. You'll update and change it as you work with your audience and members. You'll learn where they get stuck and how you can best support them on their journey. Consider this your first draft. Share it with your founding members or trusted friends and get some feedback, specifically to ensure:

- You're clear about where your audience is now and where they will be at the end of their journey
- Each stage has an empowering name and a description that captures what someone is thinking, feeling, and doing at that stage
- Each stage includes clear milestones as indicators of progress
- Each milestone has one or more action items that enable people to specifically achieve it

Your Success Path is the foundation for your content strategy, meaning the content you create inside your membership should be built around your Success Path. But what exactly will you provide? In the next chapter we'll talk about the three different types of content inside your membership site and the specific purposes they serve. So get ready, my friend! I'll see you there.

THE VALUE OF A MEMBERSHIP
DOESN'T COME FROM THE VOLUME
OF CONTENT YOU PROVIDE
IT COMES FROM THE SPEED
AT WHICH PEOPLE CAN IMPLEMENT
THE INFORMATION YOU PROVIDE

CHAPTER 24

THE THREE TYPES OF CONTENT YOU MUST HAVE

The Success Path that we just covered is the blueprint for guiding your members to the outcome they wish to achieve. Now we've got to shift gears and get into the specifics of the actual content. The big "content elephant" in the room is: What are you going to actually put inside your membership? You have to have some content for your members to consume, and it should largely be based on the structure of your Success Path.

We have to offer our customers the right information at the right time to move them toward their desired outcome. If there is no structure and everything is thrown at them at once, it creates gaps, hesitation, and lingering questions. All of which stall progress. Which leads to cancellations, the thing we're most trying to avoid. There are three different types of content that every membership should include. Each serves a different purpose and is crucial for creating an amazing member experience.

1. ONBOARDING CONTENT

The first type is called **onboarding content**. This is the content that your members see when they first join your membership. It's the warm welcome that sets the tone for their entire experience. These first few moments are critical. They frame the experience that people are going to have inside your membership. That's why it's important to map this out and get clear on the message you want to communicate. We're not dealing a lot with the Success Path here just yet, although you can reference the overall change your customers will experience. This kind of content doesn't include the "meat" of what they'll learn yet. We're just laying the groundwork.

Creating a positive onboarding experience is absolutely essential for retention. It guides your members through their initial steps and ensures that they feel confident and certain about where to go and what to do, eliminating any doubts that may arise.

A few years ago, I had a conversation with a friend who, although she had just recently joined a membership, informed me that she was already leaving it. I was taken aback and asked her why. She explained that when she logged into the membership for the first time, she felt overwhelmed and unsure of what to do or where to go. This uncertainty planted a seed of doubt in her mind about whether she could actually get the result she was after if she was already having trouble figuring out what to do first.

This is exactly what you *don't* want to happen when someone joins your membership. Unfortunately, most membership site owners forget that their job is to provide clarity. Instead, they just toss their new members into a vast library and hope that they somehow find the few nuggets that will be of value to them.

That's confusing. It also puts a lot of pressure on your member to find the value. Instead, I want *you* guiding them through how to get the most out of their membership.

And that brings me to the next element of onboarding content—holding your member's hand as they get acquainted with your membership and all the value it provides. Your goal is to help them navigate through the various sections and make it easy for them to find what they are looking for.

Here are a few specific types of onboarding content that you can include.

- **Welcome video.** While it may seem obvious, it is crucial to have a welcome video that every member will see. This video should provide a vision of the journey they are about to embark on and remind them of the benefits and reasons they joined in the first place. It also gives you the chance to set the tone and communicate the culture of your membership. By making the welcome video a mandatory part of the onboarding process, you can ensure that every member is on the same page and reminded of the purpose for your membership.
- **"Start here" section.** This section serves as a clear, practical starting point for new members to help them avoid feeling overwhelmed or unsure of where to begin. Whether it's taking a survey or watching core content, the "start here" section eliminates any guesswork and offers a clear next step.
- **Member profile.** By encouraging members to update their profiles with a picture and some information about themselves, you foster a sense of connection and community within your membership. Real people connecting with each other is far more engaging than default profile pictures. By emphasizing the importance of creating a profile, you encourage members to engage with one another and establish meaningful connections.
- **Simple membership tour.** This can be incredibly helpful in familiarizing members with the different areas and purposes within your membership. By walking members through the various sections and explaining where to find specific resources or support, you ensure that members are comfortable and can easily navigate the membership. This not only enhances their experience but also reduces the need for additional support.

- **Onboarding quiz.** Get to know where your members are in their journey so you can personalize their experience. This is a more advanced strategy made possible thanks to Membership.io. (Self-serving plug there.)

Onboarding content plays a vital role in guiding your members through their initial steps. You can ensure that your members feel confident, supported, and ready to dive into the valuable content you provide. Remember, the goal is to eliminate any uncertainties and overwhelm, and provide a seamless initial experience for your members.

2. CORE CONTENT

The second type of content is called **core content**. This is where you provide an overview of each stage of your Success Path. It's available as soon as your members join, and usually doesn't change. You can update it as needed, but often you create it once and leave it be. You can do this in a number of ways, but the simplest and most common is to provide a lesson per stage. The exact "how-to" and action items will come in the monthly content. You can also add in an "Introduction" and "Wrap-Up" lesson if you want. To use this book as an example, the five stages are the five parts and the core content is the explainer at the beginning of each chapter.

To illustrate this concept, let's map it out. If, for example, you have a 5-Stage Success Path, your core content could look like this:

Lesson 1: Introduction. Provide an overview of your Success Path and the purpose the membership provides. Tell members how they can use the following lessons to locate where they are in the journey. There's a good chance you have members at all different levels of expertise. It's important to get everybody speaking the same language and heading in the same direction.

Lesson 2: Stage 1: Describe what someone is thinking, feeling, and doing at this stage. What should their focus be at this point in their journey?

Lesson 3: Stage 2: Describe what someone is thinking, feeling, and doing at this stage. What should their focus be at this point in their journey?

Lesson 4: Stage 3: Describe what someone is thinking, feeling, and doing at this stage. What should their focus be at this point in their journey?

Lesson 5: Stage 4: Describe what someone is thinking, feeling, and doing at this stage. What should their focus be at this point in their journey?

Lesson 6: Stage 5: Describe what someone is thinking, feeling, and doing at this stage. What should their focus be at this point in their journey?

Lesson 7: Summary. Recap the Success Path and briefly touch on each lesson.

3. MONTHLY CONTENT

The third type of content is **monthly content**. This is what your members receive on a monthly basis. It's like a special gift that keeps them engaged and excited about being a member. In a publisher model, this could be fresh new content, and in a UPS model, it could be a package of content that's delivered. Whatever form it takes, the key is that it changes from month to month, keeping things interesting for your members.

For a service-based membership, the monthly, deliverable content could be a box of fresh veggies delivered each week. For a product-based membership like Dollar Shave Club, it's the monthly razors. For a community-based business, this could be a monthly co-working session, mastermind call, or one-on-one with you.

It's different from core content in that core content is an overview. It gives your members a map of where they are and where the membership will take them. Monthly content is the stuff that moves them along on that journey. This is where the rubber meets the road. When it comes to monthly content, you want to focus on one thing: getting results for your members. It's not about overwhelming them with a bunch of stuff; it's about providing them with the tools and knowledge they need to make progress along their Success Path.

Here are some ideas to get your creative juices flowing. Please know that this is like a buffet: You're not going to eat everything. Pick what works for you and your members, but don't try to do everything.

- *Coaching:* Consider offering hot seats or laser coaching sessions where you can provide personalized guidance to your members. You can also host virtual coaching sessions like webinars or Facebook Lives to answer members' burning questions.
- *Guides and Playbooks:* Create how-to guides, blueprints, playbooks, and checklists that will help your members progress along their Success Path and take action.
- *Training Archive:* Build a library of training materials that your members can access anytime. If you use a tool like Membership.io, it becomes even easier for them to find the specific videos they need.
- *Worksheets and Masterclasses:* Provide interactive worksheets and masterclasses to help your members dive deeper into specific topics. You can also invite experts to conduct interviews or teach masterclasses to add variety to your content.
- *Accountability Groups and Calls:* Foster a sense of community by offering accountability groups and regular calls where members can connect, share their progress, and support each other.

- *Challenges and Competitions:* Spice things up by organizing challenges and competitions that encourage your members to take action and achieve their goals.
- *Behind the Scenes, Blueprints or Brand Reviews, or Case Studies:* This showcases *how* someone else is using what you taught and has progressed through the various stages of your Success Path.
- *Checklists:* Create checklists so that members are better able to track their progress along their Success Path.
- *Critiques or Curated News:* Become the go-to place where people come for information in your niche so that they don't have to sift and sort through everything on their own.
- *Done-for-You:* You do the work for them so they don't have to.
- *Events:* Offer exclusive events for your members like a workshop or webinar. They can be online or offline. Coaching and/or community-based memberships do well with these.
- *Expert Interviews:* Interview industry experts and provide recordings, summaries, or transcripts of the interviews to your membership.
- *Physical Products:* People love getting stuff in the mail like mugs, backpacks, and pins. This is most appropriate for UPS model memberships.
- *Swipe Files:* People love to see examples. Swipe files are a collection of tested, proven, or existing materials such as e-mail copy, sales copy, and advertising.
- *Templates:* Take files that you use all the time, like swipe files, and turn them into templates.
- *Tools and Software:* If you can create any tools, software, or resources and offer them exclusively inside of your membership, it instantly makes your membership more valuable.

Go to predictableprofitsbook.com for more monthly content ideas.

Now let's talk about how to align your monthly content with your Success Path. You want to guide your members based on where they are in their journey. For example, if someone is in stage one, you'll recommend specific actions they should take based on the monthly content. If they're in stage five, you'll show them how to apply the content to their advanced level. Keep your finger on the pulse of your members' progress and focus on helping them move from one stage to the next. If most of your members are in the early stages, prioritize content that caters to their needs.

At the end of each deliverable, provide specific calls to action based on the different stages. This ensures that all members can apply the content in a way that's relevant to their journey. Remember, the value of your membership lies in the speed of implementation. So focus on helping your members take action and make progress.

ACTION STEPS

1. Choose your membership model: knowledge-based, community-based, product-based, service-based, or a combination.
2. Choose a content model: publisher, UPS, coaching, drip/modular model, or a combination.
3. Create your Success Path.
4. Write out your Success Path stages, milestones, and action items.
5. Create and map out all of your three content must-haves: onboarding, core, and monthly.

PART IV

CONVERT YOUR PEOPLE

This part is all about unleashing the magic that marketing can bring to your membership. It's not just about having the most incredible membership content or an awesome community. All of that is great, and of course, we want those things for sure. But here's a harsh reality: you can have the greatest membership in the world, but if nobody knows about it, then you're not going to be able to serve anyone. Marketing your membership is a necessity. You have to effectively spread the word and get your offer in front of the people who need it and will be excited about it.

One marketing strategy—just one—can flip the switch on your membership's success, transforming it from good to extraordinary. Think about Levi Kujala again, the guitar enthusiast who was doing well with his membership until he hit that all-too-familiar plateau. After joining our community, he used a specific launch strategy (that we'll talk about soon!). And guess what? Applying just that one strategy took his $30,000-a-month membership to $75,000 per month almost overnight—and now he's soaring with over 12,000+ paying members. Unbelievable, right? It's possible with strategic marketing.

Let me be real with you. The strategies we'll cover here? They're not your typical run-of-the-mill tactics. They're unique, they're unconventional, and they're designed to stand out. But most importantly, they work! These are the strategies I saw the most successful memberships using from behind the scenes at Wishlist when we powered thousands of sites. You're stepping into a gold mine of wisdom, crafted not just over years, but decades of experience in this very field. We're going to cover everything from open and closed marketing plans to nitty-gritty tactical advice for launching and relaunching. But keep in mind, it's not just about absorbing knowledge. It's about putting it into action.

Perfection? Overrated. Taking action? That's the secret sauce.

CHAPTER 25

CRAFTING AN OFFER THEY CAN'T REFUSE

How do you create an offer that will make your potential members reach into their pockets and happily hand over their credit card to join your membership? Getting people to give you their hard-earned cash is a big deal! And let me tell you, it makes marketing a heck of a lot easier if you have something that people naturally want to buy. That's what we're exploring here: the exact steps for crafting an amazing and compelling offer that's simply irresistible.

When there's a great offer on the table, people's interest naturally gets piqued. They lean in and think harder about joining your membership. Think about it like this: Have you ever walked through a grocery store and spotted your favorite blueberries on sale? Not just a tiny discount, but a whopping 50 percent off. What do you do? You load up your cart with those blueberries, of course. That's the magic of a great offer. It speaks to something inside us that says, "Hey, this deal is too good to pass up." A good offer has several key components, including a hook to grab people's attention, a perfectly positioned price point, deliverables that have meaning and purpose, as well as great bonuses and a clear call to action. Let's dig in to each one.

THE HOOK: GRABBING ATTENTION

The hook is the shiny lure that gets your audience's attention right away. It is the single statement that takes your audience from "oh, that'd be nice to have" to "I've got to have this right now!" It could appeal to their curiosity, or it could address a common problem you know your market has. No matter what, the best type of hook is one that's clear so people instantly know what's in it for them.

> ***People aren't buying the "stuff." They're buying an outcome or transformation.***

In our blueberry example, the sign that says, "Blueberries: $2 off!" instantly draws you in because you know what you're getting and why it's beneficial. You want the blueberries, and you're getting them for cheap. Your hook needs to work the same way—clear, enticing, and immediately telling people why they should care.

At the end of the day, people aren't buying the "stuff." They're buying an outcome or transformation. It is about the transformation your audience is seeking—and the hook is the promise of that transformation. Does your offer alleviate pain? Does it satisfy a deep desire? Your goal is to find a hook that speaks to the main thing your audience wants.

Hot tip: look at magazine articles for inspiration. If you do a search for "Women's Health magazine covers," you'll find tons of examples and inspiration. You could apply this to any industry magazine and get great results.

THE POWER OF CONTRAST IN PRICING

We'll get deeper into pricing in the next chapter. But for now, know that it's not just about the number—it's about the contrast.

Remember those blueberries? When you see $2 off on blueberries, it's thrilling. Because that's potentially 30 to 50 percent off. But if a car dealer told you they'd knock $2 off a car's price, you'd be like, "Seriously?"

So why is it that in one situation you're excited and the other you're almost insulted? Isn't it the same $2? It's all about the contrast! Two dollars off a $4 pint of blueberries feels a *lot* more significant than $2 off a $40,000 car. Isn't it interesting how we perceive that $2 savings so differently? That's the power of contrast. Anchor your price to something that showcases the value of what you're offering. Show your audience that it's a no-brainer investment for what they'll gain.

Another tactic is to use a pricing decoy. This is when you present customers with a few different prices in order to steer them toward a particular product. When you introduce a slightly less desirable option, another target looks more appealing. For example, if a 6-ounce cup of coffee is $2.99 and a 10-ounce cup is $7.99, you'll probably debate for a minute which one to choose. That difference in price is pretty big for a cup of coffee. But when I introduce an 8-ounce cup for $6.99, and customers can see that the difference between a medium and a large is only $1, well, that instantly makes the more expensive option more appealing. You feel like you're getting a deal!

DELIVERABLES: MORE THAN JUST STUFF

Now, let's talk about the deliverables. These are the goodies your members will get inside your membership. But please don't just share them like a shopping list. One of the biggest mistakes I see people make is talking too much about the particulars of exactly what's inside. Here's a secret: people don't care that much about *how* you deliver on the promised transformation. They just want the outcome. Remember, you're selling a transformation, not just the stuff they'll get. Connect the dots for your audience.

For every deliverable, explain why it matters. If you're offering masterclasses, templates, and checklists, explain how these will help them get closer to the result they're after. Will it save them time? Simplify a tricky task? Tell them that! It's about speed and ease. This instantly increases the value of your offer.

Don't think that your audience will automatically know the benefit. Be explicit in explaining why it matters. My little trick is to always ask myself "so what" whenever I list an item that's included in the membership. It forces me to explain why it matters. Make it crystal clear how your deliverables will make their lives better.

BONUSES: EXTRA GOODIES

Ah, bonuses. Those sweet extras that come with your offer. There are different types: *standard bonuses* and *fast action bonuses*. Standard bonuses should answer objections and help members achieve their goals faster and easier. It's like adding turbo boosters to their success journey. Fast action bonuses typically focus on helping your audience get a "quick win" and are only available for a limited time.

For The Membership Experience, I offer a lesson on "Borrowing Influence" as a standard bonus. This speaks to the common objection of "but I don't have an audience." For fast action bonuses, I offer seven-figure launch scripts, templates, and some fill-in-the-blank e-mail guides to make creating and launching a membership as simple as possible.

A CLEAR CALL TO ACTION

Are you sick of hearing this yet? Give people a call to action! Don't leave it vague. Tell people exactly what to do next! You're guiding them toward a transformation, and your call to action is the bridge to that better future. Be specific—whether it's "Join Now" or "Register Here." Clarity is a gift to your potential members. It removes guesswork and helps them take the right action now.

And that's the breakdown of crafting an irresistible offer. From positioning to pricing, each element plays a crucial role in making your membership impossible to resist. Next, I'm going to answer the question that I know is on your mind right now: *How much should I charge?*

IRRESISTIBLE OFFERS ATTRACT BUYERS

CHAPTER 26

PRICING

The million-dollar question—well, not quite a million, but you get the idea—is how much should you charge for your membership? You might also be wondering: Should you go for monthly, annual, or something completely different with your pricing? Fear not, we'll crack open the vault of pricing models and explore a variety of available options together. But before we start crunching numbers, it's important to understand one very important thing: there is no one right way to price your membership.

This isn't a one-size-fits-all approach. Yes, I'm here to guide you through these models, and yes, I'll sprinkle in a dash of bias by letting you in on my preferred options. But there is a buffet of pricing models spread out before you to choose from as it suits *you*. That's the beauty of it.

Before we get into the models, here's some general advice. When it comes to landing on an exact "number" for your membership, I recommend that you start low and gradually increase your prices. This works like the stock market, only with fewer ups and downs. Normal or average price ranges vary from market to market. Don't compare your price to someone who is in a completely different market than you. If you are helping people save money or make money, you can charge a little bit more for your front-end membership, like $50 to $100 per month. Back-end memberships (for those who have already completed a course or program of yours and are looking for more) are typically much, much higher, in the range of $200 to $1,000 per month.

It's a little bit trickier to set your pricing when your customers don't see a direct return on investment, like in hobby or pet markets. These memberships can range from just a few dollars a month to around $20 to $49 per month. Typically, you aren't going to see those markets go beyond that price point. It's not to say they can't or won't, but in general, they're under $50 per month.

Health-related markets can show a direct return on investment just by how you help people look and feel, though you have to get really good at helping people track their progress. If your customers aren't tracking their progress, they won't be able to connect the health benefits with your membership. A typical price for these is between $20 and $100 per month.

A word to the wise: start with only one membership level. I'm not a fan of throwing multiple levels into the ring from the get-go. It makes things a little more complicated for you (which takes longer to launch), and I would rather initially have one level and learn what your members want more of. Then you could easily create a second level down the road that is catered to those specific needs (and you could charge a higher price for it!). Keep it simple, and then test and experiment as you go along.

If you're a total newbie, it's even more important to start your price low. It's much easier to raise your prices than lower them. Imagine if you belonged to a membership and they said, "We're raising our prices, but your price is going to stay the same." How would you feel? Great, right? Like you made an excellent decision to join when you did. But what if they did the opposite? What if they said, "we're lowering our prices." How would you feel?

From my experience, most customers feel like they've been overpaying this whole time, and I've even seen situations where people asked for a refund for the months in which they had been paying the higher price. That's why I recommend starting with a lower price and rewarding your early adopters. Plus, coming up soon, it allows you the opportunity to leverage price increases in your marketing.

But first up, here are some common membership pricing models.

THE CLASSICS: MONTHLY AND ANNUAL

Let's start with the classics: monthly and annual. Monthly is like your old friend; it's where members pay a set fee each month for continuous access. This is how you achieve recurring revenue and predictable profits. You can also level up with annual. Here, members have the option to commit to a whole year. Generally, the incentive is a slight discount, like two months for free. Ninety-nine percent of the time, these are going to be your two main pricing models, and for good reason. It's hard to go wrong with them.

ANNUAL ONLY

But wait, there's more! There's the straight-up annual-only model, where members only have the option for a full year of membership goodness. One upfront payment for a year's worth of value—talk about commitment! We often see this for higher-priced memberships like masterminds or specialized services. But we also see it for things like Amazon Prime.

THE UPFRONT FEE PLUS MONTHLY PAYMENTS

Another option is the Upfront Fee, plus Monthly model. Members initially pay a lump sum and then continue with monthly payments. This setup can create a sense of commitment and discourage quick exits because if people leave and want to renew, they have to pay that upfront fee again. I've seen people in my community implement this when they're afraid people will come in, download everything, and then bail. But I don't want you to worry about that. You can use the upfront fee model if you want, but don't do it out of fear that people won't find enough value in your membership to stick around. The only thing to think about here is that the upfront fee will typically decrease your conversions, though it may even itself out in the long haul with the increase in retention.

THE ONE-TIME FEE—BEWARE!

Here is a pitfall I need to warn you about: the One-Time Fee model. I *do not* recommend this model because it's not really a membership if there is no recurring fee.

Trust me, I've seen the allure, but it's a broken business model—enticing at first, but you'll soon find yourself supporting more and more people without any new revenue to pay for that support. This is basically just selling a product with lots of ongoing support, but all your revenue still comes only from gaining new members. This is the exact game you're trying to stay away from.

FIXED TERMS

You may want to dip your toes into the membership world with the Fixed-Term Fee model. It's like offering a course but for a specific period, say 3, 6, or 12 months. This is great for markets that need a taste before they dive in headfirst. Sometimes prospective members are drawn to this model because it feels like there is a "finish line" within reach. Meaning, at the end of the three or six months, they'll have their outcome. With that in mind, just be careful about renewals, as they can tend to be a bit trickier.

TRIALS PLUS MONTHLY

Lastly, the Trial Plus Monthly model is your chance to let potential members test-drive the experience. With this model, a low-cost trial period, typically 3, 5, or 7 days, rolls smoothly into a full monthly membership.

Keep the number of days for the trial to a minimum. I don't recommend 30-day trials or even 14-day trials because I'd like you to begin generating revenue as quickly as possible. To get the job done, three to five days is plenty for members to get a sense of the experience you provide. And for the most part, I only recommend offering a trial *after* someone has said no to a regular promotion. Otherwise, you tend to attract people who get in and out quickly, which causes a lot of disruption.

All right, my fellow pricing pioneers, let's keep the momentum going. Pricing isn't set in stone. It's a journey of discovery and growth. Keep the enthusiasm high and the prices fair. Stay awesome, and I'll catch you in the next chapter!

CHAPTER 27

HOW TO SELL, EVEN IF YOU DON'T LIKE SELLING

Now it's time to actually sell that amazing offer you've crafted so you can make some money and start helping people. In this chapter, we are going straight into the world of copywriting—which will have your audience clicking that "Join Now" button faster than you can say "transformation." This is the language you will use when you talk about your membership anywhere you're trying to convince people to buy it: sales pages, webinars, social media, etc.

Get ready to unleash the power of your words and paint a vivid picture that your potential members can't resist. To do so, the questions you need to ask yourself are, *What do I say so that people naturally want to buy? How do I make my membership super compelling? How do I show people that what I have is valuable and they need it in their lives right now?* The answers all lie in a little skill called copywriting.

Compelling sales copy is all about creating contrast between now and the future, where it makes your audience desperate to move into their future with the help of your membership. You've already done the Messaging Map, and that's like having the blueprints for your dream home. Now, we're going to take those blueprints and turn them into a cozy, inviting space that your audience won't want to leave.

Let's use an example. Let's say you help parents navigate the sometimes turbulent waters of behavioral issues with their boys.

This is a real-world example from someone in our community, by the way. What would be in the parents' "Now" list? What are the feelings and struggles they are dealing with today? They may be thinking, "It's too late. My son will just have behavioral problems his whole life." They might be ashamed because they don't feel they have control. They avoid going out in public because they're afraid their child will burst into a tantrum and create a scene. They don't know how to move forward or who to talk to. They've looked online for ideas and strategies and are overwhelmed by all the information. Maybe they think they've tried everything already. Perhaps worst of all, they feel guilty. They're worried they've failed their child and don't know how to fix it. What can they do?

Enter: your membership. How will you help them through this? What will their life be like after your membership? Well, they'll have confidence that they can handle and navigate difficult situations with their child. They can go out in public and know what to do. They can advocate for their son and feel supported because now they'll have a community. They'll be proud of their son and feel a sense of momentum that they're both making progress. Most of all, they'll continue to develop a better, more meaningful relationship with their child. This is all essentially the Messaging Map for this membership.

You with me so far? Now, let's stitch these ideas together. If I were talking to a member of this audience, explaining the value of joining my membership, I'd say something like this:

> *If you're a parent with a son right around the age of 10, 11, or 12 who has all kinds of behavioral problems, you might be feeling that it's too late to help them, that it's a lost cause. Maybe you feel, oh my gosh, "I should have been a better parent," and you carry all of this blame on your shoulders because you have no control over your son. And it creates a scenario where you feel lonely and stuck. You avoid going out in public because you don't want to create another scene. But secretly, behind closed doors, you are researching nonstop because you're trying to figure out*

how to help your son and preserve your relationship. But everything is so incredibly overwhelming, it leaves you stuck not doing anything or experiencing any progress. And because of that, maybe you feel guilty or ashamed, and may be questioning if there is any hope to turn things around.

I've got good news. There absolutely is a way for you to be able to transform from that place of overwhelm and loneliness to a place of confidence. Where you are an advocate for your son, where you feel supported and connected with other parents who are trying to navigate the same sorts of situations, and where you have a sense of momentum because you are experiencing progress. You have a clear path, knowing exactly how to move forward, and you're proud of the progress that your son is making and that you are making in your relationship with your son. And along the way, you're trusting that the timing is right to get to that place where you no longer have the same conflict or intensity of behavioral outbursts, and where you and your son have a loving and rewarding relationship. Not only from that point, but for the many years and decades to come. If this resonates with you, then I want to invite you to join our community.

Okay, time-out. What am I doing here? I'm simply reading the words from the "Now" column and the "Future" column, stitching them together, and creating a story—the story of your potential member if they join your membership. Imagine that you're sitting across from your ideal member, sharing a cup of coffee, as you weave a tale that speaks straight to their heart and their head.

If you'd like to see some more examples of this in action, please refer to predictableprofitsbook.com.

You already have all the elements necessary to do this for your own membership. These are your building blocks, your tools. Use them wisely, mix and match, and watch the magic unfold. Imagine that you're holding a paintbrush and using words to create a vivid picture of where your potential member is right now. Be descriptive, make them nod along, thinking, *Yes, that's exactly how I feel.* Then paint the picture of their potential future. The secret to effortless selling is not just creating copy but guiding your potential members toward a decision that will change their lives. Be confident, be their mentor. Let them know that you understand where they are and that you have the solution they've been waiting for.

Your words have the potential to resonate deep within your audience, stirring emotions and driving action. Don't rush this process. Take your time with crafting the copy. Make every word count. Your words are the bridge between where your potential members are now and the transformation your membership offers. The key to writing compelling copy is to create contrast and a gap between where they are and where they want to be. When that gap is clear, your membership becomes the obvious next step

Armed with your Messaging Map and the power of compelling copy, you're prepared to create a sales page that sings. Let's keep those words flowing!

CHAPTER 28

SALES PAGE FUNDAMENTALS

With your compelling copy and the beautiful future you painted for your potential customers, it's time to give them a way to actually join your membership! Creating a high-converting sales page is one of the most crucial aspects of this process. Your sales page is the window through which your audience peers into your offer, and when you get it right, it can be a game-changer for your business. This is where potential members will make the decision to join your community or not. It's a big deal, so let's be intentional about it.

Think of your sales page as a journey, a series of sections that guide your reader toward that "join now" button. Here is the basic structure: you have a headline, a sub-headline, a bit of copy, and then a new section. Rinse and repeat, with headlines and copy throughout. This structure allows your readers to skim and still understand what you're offering, how it benefits them, and why it's a no-brainer. People are short on time and often won't read every single word on the page, so you need to make sure the important information is obvious for the skimmers.

SEVEN CRITICAL QUESTIONS

To craft an effective sales page, you need to answer seven essential questions for your customers. Let's break them down one by one.

1) What Are You Offering?

Right out of the gate, you need to clearly state your offer. This is your hook, the problem that you solve. Talk about your membership, your community, and the transformation you provide. Make it crystal clear what you are making available to them.

2) Why Does It Matter?

This is what they're really after. What's at stake if they don't solve this problem or challenge right now? Will the problem or challenge get worse? Will their desired future get farther and farther away? Talk about the internal problems of your potential customer and connect the dots for them.

For example, in a parenting membership, it matters because if you don't fix things now, your kids could be screwed up for life! (Kidding . . . but not kidding.) If people don't sign up for your healthy meal-planning membership, they'll keep eating out and potentially wasting money and negatively affecting their health. If people don't join your dog-breeding membership, they'll make a mistake that could hurt both their business and the dogs. Make it crystal clear why your membership matters.

3) Who Are You?

People want to know your backstory. Did you discover a solution yourself? Experience the transformation yourself? Or have you helped others do it? Share how you came up with this offer. Whether it's your personal journey or another story, they've got to know why *you* are the one who can help them experience the transformation they're after.

4) What Is Possible?

Paint a vivid picture of what's possible once someone joins your membership. This is where capturing your customers' success stories comes into play. Share stories of real people, just like your potential members, who've experienced transformation. Show, don't just tell. People want to see other *real* people, just like them, who have been where they currently are and experienced the transformation you are promising. This is also a great place to showcase your Success Path.

5) What's Included?

List out what your membership offers. Highlight your core content and monthly deliverables. But don't stop there; explain why each element matters and what it will make possible for your members.

6) What Is the Price?

Don't be shy about pricing. Be confident and clear about it. Share why it's an incredible deal. Break down the price so they can clearly see how the value you're going to provide will far exceed their investment (e.g., you will get XYZ for less than $0.50 a day).

7) What's the Next Step?

Wrap it all up by making it clear and overt: you want them to click that "join now" button. Don't leave any room for confusion.

All you need to do now is take each of these questions and create a headline or quick line that answers it. Add in a little bit of the compelling "Now/Future" copy you created in Chapter 29 and create a flow walking people through the answers to these questions. Essentially, we want to create a headline that speaks directly to each question, and then have copy underneath that provides a little more context. You can mix up the order if you want, but make sure you address each question. If you skip one, you will leave a gap in the mind of your audience, whether consciously or subconsciously, and they won't take the action you want. But if you hit all of these points, then you will have a compelling sales page, your audience will "get it," and conversions will soar.

Here are a few more quick tips:

- Ensure your sales page is mobile-friendly. People use their phones more than ever these days, and your page needs to be both legible and functional on mobile devices.
- Keep the headlines and subheads interesting. If you don't capture your audience's attention and give them a reason to stay on your page, they'll bounce.
- The reader should be able to easily move from section to section, getting the essence of what you do, what you provide, and how that makes their life better.

With your sales page in place, you're ready to launch, right? You can launch ineffectively or super effectively. I hope so. That's why we're now going to explore the secrets of a super effective launch in the next chapter.

To see lots of examples of sales pages that do exactly this, visit predictableprofitsbook.com.

CHAPTER 29

TWO KINDS OF MARKETING PLANS

It's time to jump into something different and juicy in this chapter. We're going to talk about the difference between an Open Marketing Plan, which means keeping the "doors" open day in and day out, and a Closed Marketing Plan, where you only let people join your membership during certain times and close the doors otherwise.

You might be thinking, "Well, of course, Stu, I want my membership open all the time. Isn't that the point?" I get it, at first glance, why wouldn't you want to keep the doors open and let people join whenever they want? But hold your horses, because there are plenty of reasons to go with the Closed Marketing Plan instead. But let's first focus on the Open Plan, because it's the one that often gets the most spotlight.

The Open Marketing Plan shines when you have a membership in a market where your audience craves instant access. There are lots of markets where your customers need help immediately. Like moms who are about to give birth. They're not keen on waiting around. Or people in debt who need help now or anyone trying to make a career change or solve an immediate health issue. All of these people are looking for help right here, right now.

Back in the day, when I was at the helm of WishList Member, we realized that in addition to getting tech support for creating their membership, folks also wanted to learn marketing and strategy.

So we created a membership that was dedicated to helping other membership owners grow their membership (talk about meta!). Initially, we had an Open Marketing Plan, and it started strong. But we plateaued after a while and had trouble enrolling people. This is a common problem for memberships with the Open Marketing Plan experience.

Having your doors open 24/7 is all well and good, but your marketing can't just be a passive "come join whenever." You need to stir up some urgency. Otherwise people will "save it for later." And you know what that means, right? Yup, it means they're likely never coming back.

So how do you create a sense of urgency when you're open all the time? My recommendation is to create 12 irresistible bonuses or promotions. Then, each month, you roll out one of these bonuses and make it available to new sign-ups if they register before a certain deadline. For example, say your membership is $20 a month, and each of these bonuses is worth $97. Bam! The moment someone sees that they're thinking, *Hey, I can snag this $97 value for just $20 this month.* And that's where the urgency kicks in. You're not only opening your doors, but you're offering a cherry on top that's too good to resist.

> ***The first goal is to give them a reason to join.***

Now, I can hear your skepticism—it's echoing in my ears. "But Stu, won't they just join for the bonus and then bail?" No way. Think of it this way: Sure, they may come for the bonus initially, and that's okay. But you're going to rock their world with the value you provide. The first goal is to give them a reason to join. But they'll stay for all the other benefits—the community, the content, and the transformation you're offering. The bonus is just the golden ticket that gets them through the door.

And here's a hot tip: treat your existing members like royalty too. Any new bonus you roll out, give it to them as well. It's a retention tactic that'll keep your following engaged and excited. Because it's not just about getting them in—it's about wowing them once they're here. Just make sure you communicate about it and build up excitement with your existing members. And don't worry, you don't have to reinvent the wheel every year. Those bonuses can make their comeback, year after year.

Next up, let me ask you something: Do you want to make more money while working less? If so, welcome to the world of the Closed Marketing Plan, where we flip the script and do something that seems counterintuitive but brings incredible results. This plan involves periodically closing the doors on your membership so that people *can't* register. Then a few times a year you open the doors where they can join for a limited period of time (usually 5 to 7 days). When you do this, it creates a real sense of urgency for people to join during your registration periods.

I know the Closed Marketing Plan might sound like I've been sipping on some wild concoction. Why would you ever want to close the doors to your membership, right? Well, let me tell you the story of how this all clicked for me.

Back in the day, when I was business partners with Michael Hyatt and we were launching his membership, Michael had readers who absolutely adored his *New York Times* best-selling book, *Platform: Get Noticed in a Noisy World*, and were hungry for more. So we launched a membership and went all in with the Open Marketing Plan, including promotions every month, creating that buzz and urgency.

It was working great. We were welcoming around 100 to 125 new members each month. But like all good tales, there's a twist. Michael started feeling a bit claustrophobic with our marketing calendar. He wanted room to breathe, share other offers, and really go deep with his audience.

So we switched gears, closed the doors, and in our very first closed promotion, we added over 600 new members. A total game-changer. With the Open Marketing Plan, we'd welcomed about 1,500 new members per year. But with the Closed Marketing Plan, using four promotions a year, we welcomed around 2,400 members for the year. That meant less effort and more results. It was a beautiful thing.

But just when you thought the numbers couldn't get any better, brace yourself. We went all in with only two promotions a year. And guess what? Even *more* magic happened. We now welcomed around 1,500 to 2,000 members with each promotion. So again, with half the number of promotions, we were welcoming more total members each year (now 3,000 to 4,000 new members). The membership floodgates had burst open.

You, too, can have a bigger impact while still having time to sip your morning coffee without the chaos of constant promotions. Sounds dreamy, doesn't it? It's the equivalent of discovering a cheat code for growing your membership.

Not convinced? You should know by now what's coming next: let's talk success stories. Jennifer Allwood is a go-getter and an action-taker who teaches Christian women how to build online businesses. When I met her, she had a membership that just wasn't growing as quickly as she wanted. It took her three years to get to roughly 700 members, which was solid growth, but she knew she was capable of more. Now I'll admit, she was very reluctant to close her doors. But to her credit, she was open to learning. My advice was, "Worst-case scenario, if it doesn't work out the way you want, you can always open it back up." So she went for it. Using the Closed Marketing Plan, she welcomed over 1,100 new members in a single promo.

Ali Kay was doing well by keeping her painting membership open. She had welcomed roughly 1,400 members over a two-year period. Then she decided to try closing her membership to create space on her marketing calendar and utilized a "coaching week" promotion. With that one promotion, she welcomed more than 3,000 *new* members! Here are screenshots of some of her updates that she was leaving in our community as it was happening in real time:

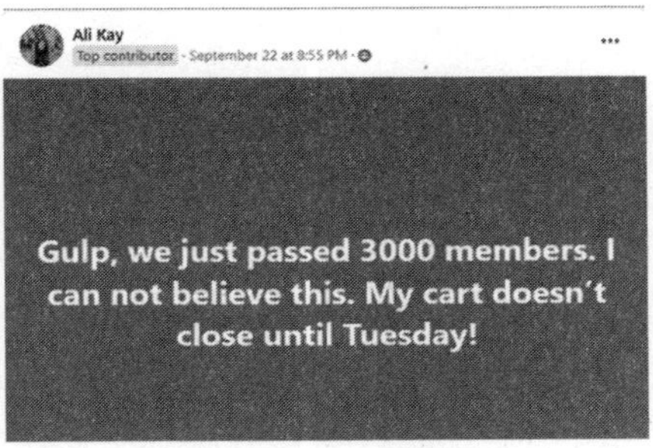

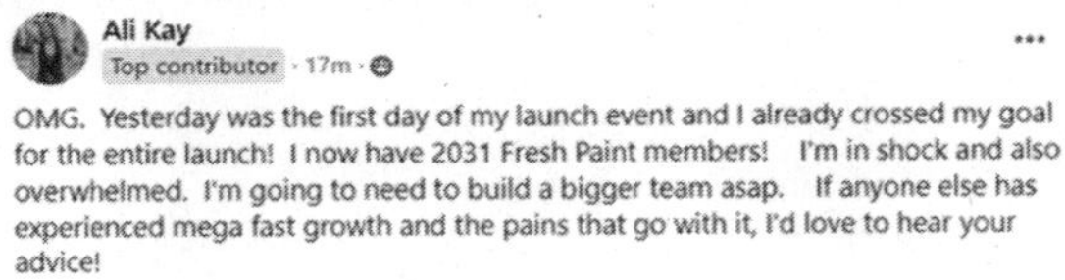

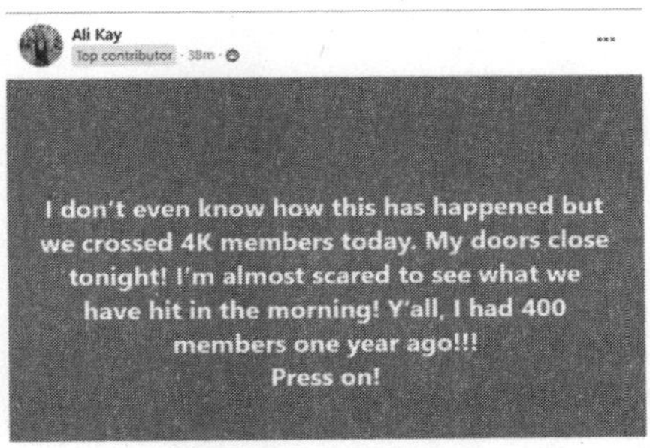

I'm not just blowing hot air here. This plan works, and it works wonders. Especially in the early stages when you're still setting up shop, the Closed Marketing Plan can be your secret sauce.

All right, my friend. I know you're probably anxious to launch your membership into the world, so let's get to it. Next up, we'll lay the groundwork for having your biggest membership launch ever and welcoming more members than you ever dreamed possible.

CHAPTER 30

MASTERING THE 5 PHASES OF LAUNCH SUCCESS

Let me tell you, I've got plenty of experience in the world of multimillion-dollar launches. I've been around the block, and I've learned a thing or two. But there's one thing I want you to remember: the longer the runway, the bigger the launch. Think about that for a minute. A longer lead-up to your launch means more time to create connection, awareness, anticipation, and excitement. You know I love a scrappy, use-what-you've-got-and-start-now kinda launch. That's basically what our founding member launch is for! But right now, we are going bigger. This is about the launches that come after that.

For the first 10 years in my business, I thought I was following the right launch process by delivering a series of valuable content, where people would see the value in what I was sharing and therefore join me in whatever I was offering. But after I met Jeff Walker, I discovered I was missing a critical concept—the psychology behind each piece of content and how they all connect. Regardless of whether you're using scripted, pre-recorded videos or if you're live streaming your launch, understanding the psychology of it all is absolutely essential. It took me a while to see this. But over time, with each launch and a commitment to mastering the art of launching, I moved from four-figure launches to seven-figure launches.

Now I can proudly say that I've executed 18 multimillion-dollar launches. Yes, that's a lot, but what's even more exciting is that the launch fundamentals I used have also worked wonders for members of our community, enabling them to achieve five-, six-, and seven-figure launches themselves. I credit Jeff with truly pioneering the online launch. He literally wrote the *New York Times* best-selling book *Launch*. He has had a profound ripple effect in my life (and now the lives of so many in our community). With that said, people often make the mistake of misunderstanding the purpose of each element in a launch.

> ***The longer the runway, the bigger the launch.***

Yes, each component has to do with content. But it's the way in which the psychology is blended with the content, along with the timing of the sequence. The five phases outlined here are my own interpretation of Jeff's incredible launch formula, blended with my "simple Stu" wisdom.

Imagine these five phases as a timeline. Notice that the time between each phase gets shorter as we approach the launch date. Let's break them down.

PHASE 1: THE CONNECTION PHASE (AT LEAST 1 MONTH IF POSSIBLE)

The first phase is all about building a deep connection with your audience—both in their minds and their hearts. Remember when we talked about clarifying your values and beliefs? Remember my example of Gary Vee glorifying working on Christmas Eve and how it rubbed me the wrong way? In that moment I got tremendous clarity around the fact that I *don't* agree with the hustle, hustle, hustle culture. When I shared my reaction video about how much I value family and a different pace of life, it really resonated with my audience. Both in their minds and on a deeper, emotional level.

I created contrast between the current reality of hustle culture and missing out on time with family, and the future reality with a more manageable pace of life, more freedom, and more time with loved ones. The goal during the connection phase is to connect with your audience around values, beliefs, and your philosophy.

PHASE 2: THE AWARENESS PHASE (2–4 WEEKS)

After you've made a connection with your audience, it's time to create awareness about what's possible with your membership and take the relationship to the next level. Share stories of individuals at various stages of their journey along your Success Path. Plant the seed of curiosity in your audience's mind, making them wonder if they could achieve similar results. You may have heard me say this before (like a million times!), but you've got to tell good success stories and show your audience what's possible. Big wins, little wins, and everything in between. These stories make the transformation seem attainable, and people will naturally lean in and want to learn more—especially when they can see themselves in the stories you're sharing. That's why it's important to share a variety of stories of people who have all kinds of different characteristics and attributes. Young, old, experienced, brand-new, with different skills or life circumstances—the more variety, the more likely people will find a story that resonates with themselves.

I like to share stories of people who didn't have an audience or e-mail list when they were just getting started, like Joy Anderson or Sarah Williams. There's also Lauren Kelly, who didn't even know what a membership was when she joined our community. Then she welcomed 14 founding members to her piano teacher membership and did an even bigger launch a few months later, welcoming 49 members—all with just about zero online presence and e-mail list at the beginning. Their stories feel *way* more within reach than stories of people adding thousands of members to an already established membership.

But does that mean you don't share those stories? Not at all. Because those stories are going to appeal to a different type of person. For example, Gabby Bernstein is a very established business owner and *New York Times* best-selling author. When Gabby and I first met, she had a membership for years that had plateaued at around 1,100 members. And when I share the story of her team flying up to Toronto and redesigning her launch during a day of consulting, resulting in more than 4,500 new members, it resonates for the person who has a membership that's not quite performing at the level they want and are realistically able to obtain.

Both stories are important because they appeal to different segments of my audience. Similarly, you will have different segments of your audience. It's also a good idea to think through the objections your audience has and make content to specifically address them. That way, when you begin to sell to them, you've already removed any blocks or arguments they might have.

PHASE 3: THE DESIRE PHASE (1–2 WEEKS)

Phase three is what most people think of when it comes to online product launches. It's the desire phase, where you shift gears and focus on the offer you're going to make. This is where you generate maximum momentum. The key is to build anticipation and desire for your offer. The longer you've spent in the connection and awareness phases, the more momentum you'll have heading into the desire phase. This lasts about one to two weeks, where people are given the opportunity to sign up for the membership. You need to create a buzz and make it crystal clear that joining your membership is the fast track to transformation.

Jeff Walker calls this the "opportunity." Any content you create has to cast a grand vision of what life will be like in the future when your audience embraces what you're about to share. Circle back to your Messaging Map and outline where your market is now and where they want to be. Then paint a vivid picture of the future your audience wants. That future is the opportunity. Make it clear what's possible if they join your membership.

In my case, I talk about the shift from the old way of doing business (relying on one-time transactions) to the new way (establishing recurring revenue through memberships). I discuss what this transition can mean for business owners and those they serve (less stress, more stability, and more predictability in their business). The key is creating a contrast between the two worlds and helping your audience imagine what life could be like if they embrace your teachings.

The second key revolves around helping your audience experience a transformation right from the start. Think of it as setting them on a path to a brighter future. Identify a small milestone within your Success Path that can create immediate momentum or provide clarity. For me, if I can help someone create a powerful Messaging Map, or even welcome their first member through a founding member launch, it creates massive momentum for them very early on.

Sharing stories of individuals one step ahead of your audience can also be incredibly impactful by making the transformation feel attainable. (Yes, stories, stories, stories in every phase of the launch.) Big wins are great, but they can feel out of reach. It's the people who are *just* a touch ahead of you that make progress feel possible. That's why in any launch we design, we want to teach content that helps our audience feel like they've already made progress toward the future they desire.

Christie Hawkins does this for her painting membership by walking her audience through painting a beginner-level project. When they complete the painting, they can see the progress they've already made and feel the momentum on their side. Susan Garrett does this by helping her audience of dog owners with some basic training games. After a couple of days practicing these games, her audience begin to see the progress in their dog's behavior. That's a major step toward their desired future of a well-trained dog. John Michaloudis has a membership teaching advanced techniques for using Microsoft Excel. During his launch, he shows how to do a couple of calculations that his audience can immediately start using. These are super powerful because they "excel-lerate" the progress of the people consuming his launch materials (sorry, #DadJoke). But you get my point.

Another Jeff Walker term I want to introduce you to here is "the blueprint." This is where you zoom out and offer a high-level overview of all the different things that go into experiencing the transformation. This incentivizes people to work with you because they see the bigger picture and have a deeper understanding of what it's going to take to get that outcome, all while reducing their learning time. They want you to walk them through your whole process. They don't just want to know what to do, but *how* to do it. And this is where your membership becomes the solution.

Never ever worry about giving away too much value in this process. People always tell me they're worried that if they say all of this during their launch no one will sign up for the membership because they'll already have everything they need! Nothing could be further from the truth. Just take this book, for example. Between what's in the book and the extra bonuses I've shared, you could 100 percent take these materials and launch a super successful membership. But there will be some people (maybe you?) who will want to go deeper or get additional support as you implement. From my experience, lead with generosity. Most people will be drawn to you and will want more. During this all-important desire phase, think through these questions:

1. What is the opportunity for my audience?
2. How will their life be better or different?
3. What will be possible after experiencing the transformation we provide?
4. What evidence or proof can I share to show that this transformation is happening for others?
5. What is a quick win I could help my audience achieve?
6. What would feel like early progress toward the bigger outcome?

7. How could I accelerate someone's progress in a simple way?
8. What would create momentum for someone starting today?
9. How could I visually provide a high-level overview of the Success Path?
10. What does the long-term plan look like?
11. What are the few key areas that are essential for long-term success?

Remember, this phase is just about creating desire for your membership, and we're not quite opening the cart yet. That's next.

PHASE 4: THE PURCHASE PHASE (4–7 DAYS)

The fourth phase is the purchase phase, or the open cart phase. This is when you open the doors for people to purchase your product. Keep this phase relatively short—it's where you capitalize on the momentum you've built. I like to keep my cart open window pretty tight as I know that the longer it's open, the more momentum wanes. That's why my open cart period is typically 4 to 5 days. Think of this as a big crescendo building up to this point. All the sales (and magic) happen during this period.

PHASE 5: THE WOW PHASE (ONGOING. NEVER STOP WOWING!)

Finally, we've got the wow phase! This is where you focus on delivering your offer. You've closed your cart, welcomed members, and now it's time to make their first few weeks with you a huge success. Your goal? Knock their socks off. Make sure your members have an outstanding experience, achieve incredible results, and become raving fans. You're already set them up to do this since you created a stellar membership and hopefully have some great results already through your founding member launch. This amazing experience in your membership really matters. It sets your members up for success, helps them get results, and sets you up for more amazing launches.

Now, I know you're probably wondering about timing, and I've got you covered. Whether you have more or less time, here is a sample timing plan, which can be adjusted to suit your particular business needs.

Plan 1: The Super Whiz-Bang Launch (All-In)

Pre-April 4: Warm up your audience

April 4: Membership Guide (entire list)

April 7: Membership Guide (unopens)

April 10: Strategies and Tactics From the Pros: Membership Tips (entire list)

April 12: Strategies and Tactics From the Pros: Membership Tips (unopens)

April 14: Promote Membership Workshop—Turn What You Already Know, Love, and Do into a Profitable Membership (entire list)

April 17: Promote Membership Workshop— Turn What You Already Know, Love, and Do into a Profitable Membership (unopens)

April 19: Promote Membership Workshop— Turn What You Already Know, Love, and Do into a Profitable Membership (nonclicks)

April 20: Promote Membership Workshop/Last Chance to Register/Starts Tomorrow— Turn What You Already Know, Love, and Do into a Profitable Membership (nonclicks)

April 21 A.M.: Membership Workshop Part 1 (entire list)

April 21 P.M.: Membership Workshop Part 1 Replay (unopens)

April 22 A.M.: Membership Workshop Part 2 (entire list)

April 22 P.M.: Membership Workshop Part 2 Replay (unopens)

April 23 A.M.: Membership Workshop Part 3 (entire list)

April 23 P.M.: Membership Workshop Part 3 Replay/Webinar Tomorrow (unopens)

April 24: Webinar Today

April 25 A.M.: Cart Open/Early Bird Bonus + Encore Webinar at 3 P.M. (entire list)

April 25 P.M.: Cart Open/Early Bird Bonus (engaged contacts or entire list)

April 26 A.M.: Heads Up About Livecast Tonight (engaged contacts or entire list)

April 26 (15 mins before going live): Live Starting Soon. (engaged contacts or entire list)

Pro tip: After your launch, I recommend conducting a quick debrief for yourself and/or your team so you can continue to do it even better next time. This allows you to reflect on your experience and learn from both your wins and your areas for improvement.

The act of filling them in will help you internalize these fundamentals and five phases of launching.

For some simple launch templates that will help you outline for your e-mails, website copy, audios, videos, etc., visit predictableprofitsbook.com.

In a launch, there aren't any standalone components. To achieve success, they need to work together seamlessly. This is your road map to launch success. Keep your energy up, stay positive, and let's make your membership dreams a reality!

THE LONGER THE RUNWAY THE BIGGER THE RESULTS

CHAPTER 31

FINDING YOUR LAUNCH STYLE

There are countless ways to launch a membership, but the key to doing it successfully is to find what feels right for you and resonates with your audience. So let's discover the launch style that aligns perfectly with you.

For the record, I *love* launching. However, I've come to realize that not everyone feels the same or wants to follow the exact same script. Some people may not be at ease in front of a camera, while others might thrive in a live setting. And when you try to follow a method that doesn't feel natural or right to you, you end up avoiding it and not taking any action. I don't want that happening for you. The truth is, there's no one-size-fits-all approach to launching, but each method builds on the fundamentals.

When we talk about your Launch Style, we're not just talking about comfort levels. We're also talking about your ability to get creative within the framework of launching. There's a wide spectrum, ranging from super minimalist launches to elaborate, all-the-bells-and-whistles launches. The key is finding your sweet spot within this spectrum.

No matter your comfort level, I encourage you to err on the side of simplicity. Why? Because simplicity leads to action, and action leads to learning. The more you launch, the more you'll discover about positioning your offer and communicating its transformation.

With that, let's explore two ends of the spectrum: the Super Minimalist Launch and the Super Whizz-Bang Launch.

THE SUPER MINIMALIST LAUNCH

Remember Anna Saucier who did a founding member launch with a tiny audience of just 326 people? She is the perfect example of a Super Minimalist Launch. This could look like putting up a simple Facebook post with a call to action asking people to send a direct message if they're interested in joining. Then when they do, you send them a PayPal link to register. I get so much pushback when I talk about this because people assume it's too simple. But it's not! I've seen it work over and over again. Anna ended up generating over $5,000 in that one weekend. No sales page, no funnels, no bells and whistles. Simple, effective, and proof that less can be more.

A step up from that might be an e-mail promotion with a variety of messages with some social media posts sprinkled in for good measure. This is relatively straightforward, but as you see, the more elements that you add, the more complex it becomes. This is why keeping things simple is very important—especially in the beginning.

THE SUPER WHIZZ-BANG LAUNCH

On the other end of the spectrum, we have the Super Whizz-Bang Launch, where you pull out all the stops. It includes everything from webinars and videos to e-mail sequences and live events. That's what I do with The Membership Experience. It's a huge week-long launch that we only do once a year. But here's the thing: this level of complexity is something you'll work up to over time. We didn't start out doing it like this; we learned along the way.

Let me share a few success stories to illustrate the range of launch styles. Wendy Batten offers a membership that helps paint-store retailers run their businesses. It's a super niche market. When she began, she had only 453 paint-store owners in her audience.

To launch, she simply used a few Facebook Lives and e-mails over several days and ended up welcoming 59 founding members and generating just over $2,800 in recurring revenue. Scarlett Cochran is a finance and wealth expert who founded the website One Big Happy Life. Through that, she created her membership, the Wealth Builders Society, which gives students a structured approach to building wealth. She started with a founding member launch consisting of a few e-mails that she sent to a small group of 300 people, and she gained 30 founding members. A few months later, she expanded the launch to her whole audience and added things like videos and webinars, and through those efforts she now has thousands of members.

Even someone as accomplished as *New York Times* best-selling author Kris Carr had to step out of her comfort zone. I encouraged Kris to use live webinars in her launches for *years*, and when she finally did, she drastically improved her conversion rate.

Your Launch Style should align with what feels natural to you. It's essential to start where you're comfortable and progressively incorporate new strategies, whether it's video, audio, text, or live broadcasts. Pushing your limits can yield incredible results, and you can always change your launch plan and strategy to match your comfort level with wherever you are at while keeping it simple and effective. In the next chapter, we'll break down specific tactics that can be combined to formulate an entire launch.

CHAPTER 32

12 PROVEN PROMOTIONAL TACTICS AND STRATEGIES FOR MEMBERSHIP GROWTH

So what do you actually *do* to launch your membership? You now know the five phases—connection, awareness, desire, purchase, and wow—and that you can go big or go small. Now it's time to get into the nuts and bolts of the tactics and strategies you can use to create excitement, teach your audience, and sell your membership. You'll primarily implement these during the awareness and desire phases of your launch. But you can also choose one or two to throw in in-between big launches for an influx of sales/cash if you want to.

Now let's imagine your launch as a buffet. There are *tons* of different options you can offer. If you're doing a huge Super Whizz-Bang Launch, maybe you'll pick six different food items (strategies/tactics). If it's a Super Minimalist Launch, maybe just two or three. This is where things get really fun. Let's lay out your options and find the combo that works best for you and your audience. There's no one-size-fits-all answer, because it all depends on your unique circumstances, launch style, and available resources. If you're a solopreneur, you might keep it simple. But if you have some assistance, like a team or an assistant, you can experiment with a more elaborate launch recipe.

Founding Member Launch: Remember, we covered this in Chapter 16. This is your inaugural launch. This is the simplest strategy to use for initially getting your membership going because it consists of one carefully crafted message that can be posted on social media, delivered via e-mail, or even shared in video or audio.

Flash Sales: What about those moments in between bigger launches? How do you keep the momentum sizzling? (And potentially increase your monthly revenue by *a lot.*) That's where the flash sale promo comes into play. It's like a mini-explosion of excitement. Let's say you have a waitlist of eager potential members. All you're doing with this promotion is sending them a private invitation to register. So if they go to your main website, they will see that the membership is closed. But because they are on the e-mail waitlist, they have an exclusive opportunity to register. Usually the registration window is very short (1 to 2 days) and the whole promotion is delivered via e-mail. Hit them with an exclusive offer that's too good to resist.

Scott Paley, who you heard about before, uses flash sales to consistently welcome 300 to 500 new members each time. A simple e-mail promo can contain as few as three to five e-mails with the first e-mail being delivered a few days before the opening. The remaining e-mails are more specific in directing people to where they can register. The best part is you can reuse the same e-mail campaign each time you decide to run a flash sale promo.

Trials: Trials are when you give people access to your membership for a very, very low price like $1. Typically, the access is for a short period of time (1 to 2 days). Now, this might sound intriguing, and they can be effective, but here's the deal: you want to tread carefully here. Trials can be a mixed bag. While they might get more people in the door, be prepared for a higher turnover rate. Think of it as a short-term relationship—some will stick around, but if the membership isn't positioned properly, a lot of those new members won't, at least not for very long. That being said, there's no denying they can be useful, especially on the back end of a public promo for anyone who didn't register through the initial ones.

As an example, after one of our relaunch promotions with Michael's Platform University, we decided to run a trial offer for everyone who didn't initially purchase during the promotion. Ballpark math, we welcomed roughly 700 new members through the trial and 400 of them decided to stay after the trial was complete. In our minds, that was a *huge* win because those roughly 400 people had initially decided *not* to join. But because we offered the trial, it gave them a chance to experience the value of the membership. Give people a taste, and they might just fall in love.

Kelly Tay of Juicy Parenting did something similar. Her membership helps Asian parents leave old-school discipline behind. Kelly had 125 people join her for a trial membership, and 80 converted into paying members. That's a 64 percent conversion. This method definitely works. Just make sure your offer is positioned properly.

Evergreen: This is where you allow people to join your membership on an ongoing basis. For example, you might advertise on Facebook, where the ads lead people to a webinar. During the webinar, you then offer people a chance to register for your membership. And this evergreen funnel works 24/7. It's like a sidekick that complements your main promotions. If people went to your main website, they would not be able to register. When they come through this evergreen funnel, they have a few days where they can register through a special link.

Evergreen can be a powerhouse, but I'd suggest saving it for when your membership is well-established, typically after hitting that 2,000- to 3,000-member mark. The reason is that evergreen promotions require a lot more of an investment in ads. Your messaging and marketing really need to be dialed in—otherwise it's not profitable to scale the ads. But when you have those things dialed in, an evergreen promotion can be one of the most effective ways to scale from a few thousand members to tens of thousands.

Joint Venture (JV) Promotions: As you know by now, the fastest way to grow your list is to get in front of other people's audiences. Well, friends, you're going to want to do that again here. The fastest way to biggie size your launch is with something called a joint venture, where you have affiliates who receive a commission when someone from their audience buys. It's normally in the neighborhood of 20 to 30 percent on a monthly, recurring basis. Since these strategic partners make money from your launch, they're motivated to promote it, providing you with a virtual sales force. This could be a one-off promotion (like a simple e-mail blast they send to their e-mail list) or it could be part of any other promotion you run where your affiliates are sending their audience to your offer. Here's a quick checklist for the support you can offer to your affiliate to help you run a great joint venture.

Keys to Effective Affiliate Support

- Do the thinking for them. Provide promotional calendars to make it easy for them to fit your promotion into their schedule.
- Provide plenty of tools and swipe files. Create e-mail templates, social media templates, anything that they may use to promote your membership.
- Communicate often. Communicate on a regular basis. The volume of that communication should pick up as you move through the different phases of your launch.

Challenge: A challenge is a fantastic way to generate excitement leading up to your open cart. It walks people through the initial steps of experiencing a small transformation, setting the stage for a more significant change if they follow your Success Path. Challenges can be three to seven days long, creating momentum before the offer. The focus is to help people experience a "step" toward their final outcome. If you have a membership around exercise, maybe you have people work out for five days in a row or get outside every day for a week. You want people to feel some momentum after completing the challenge. Then, toward the end of the challenge, you're offering people the chance to continue that momentum by joining your membership.

Coaching Week: Innovated by our community member Sarah Williams, a coaching week is more interactive and involves teaching and coaching. Typically, you would teach some core lessons and walk people through a process for something you might cover in your membership. A great example might be covering a lesson that would lead to your audience achieving a small "milestone" in your Success Path. Then, throughout the coaching week, you would offer people the opportunity to join your membership. These are similar to a Challenge. However, the major difference is that you would have a lot more of "you" coaching people and guiding people in a group setting.

Ali Kay charges $10 for her coaching week (which helps her pay for her ads), and she then uses that to incentivize people to join her membership by giving them a $10 credit toward the first month of their membership.

Video Series: This was popularized by my buddy Jeff Walker. It's a series of three videos that can be used to guide your audience through understanding the opportunity, knowing the first steps they can take as well as getting a high-level overview of your Success Path. The videos usually lead to a webinar where you then make your offer. Remember, the more value you provide during the three videos, the more people will want to join you inside your membership. Each piece of content must position the opportunity and the transformation, as Jeff explains it.

My team and I used this message successfully for years and years, though we pivoted during COVID because we realized the tone of those prerecorded videos was off considering the state of the world. Instead, we tweaked the content and delivered it live. To our surprise, it converted even higher. That's how we discovered that, for us, live videos converted even better!

Live Broadcast: Going live can be a game-changer. It creates a sense of urgency, authenticity, and interaction with your audience. But it does add pressure, as there's not a lot of room for mistakes; there's no going back if you mess up. You might not want to use live video on your very first launch and wait until you've built up a little experience first. But I do want to encourage you to try it sooner rather than later. You could start by doing some live Q&As. The live format may work better for certain audiences, and the only way to know is to try it. But the core of the strategy here is to replicate the messaging that you might use in a prerecorded video series, except you simply deliver it live.

Webinars: Webinars bring everything together and provide a perfect platform for making your offer. They have long been a successful tool for gaining early momentum during the open cart period. They're also great for converting people into buyers because you're able to convey a lot in a short period of time. And when you combine the information with interactivity, it really engages people to take action—especially when you make your offer at the end. This one's tried and true. My buddy Russell Brunson has mastered this format. If you do a search for his perfect webinar, you'll find his structure.

Social Media: Utilize your social media channels to communicate, create anticipation, and get people excited about your launch. Every platform you use should be synchronized with your launch messaging.

Paid Ads: Paid advertising can be the fuel that propels your launch forward because it allows you to reach a broader audience. Ensure that your ad messaging aligns with your launch strategy to avoid confusion.

A quick note on this: I see lots of entrepreneurs and marketers bragging about how they only use organic traffic. And don't get me wrong, organic traffic is great. But we want all that we can get. If you could spend $1 on an ad to acquire a customer that pays you $2, how often would you do that? All day long, right? My point is that ads are an awesome way to amplify what you're already doing. They enable us to get in front of more people. Sure, there's a learning curve. And there are other experts who specialize in and can teach you that.

But when you know you have a great product and can serve people well, consider pouring a little gas on the fire with paid ads.

To wrap it all up, my friend, you've got an array of strategies and tactics at your fingertips; each has its place in your marketing arsenal. If you're just starting, the founding member launch is your go-to. If you're growing, consider incorporating some of the other elements into your next promotion and launch. Trials can be intriguing, but mind the turnover and set appropriate expectations. And if you're further down the road, dip your toes into the evergreen waters.

Now I know that after you have all of these amazing people in your membership, you want to know how to keep them around for months and years to come. That's up next. There's a lot more goodness coming your way.

ACTION STEPS

1. Choose a price and create your irresistible membership offer.
2. Build your sales page based on the seven critical questions.
3. Decide on your marketing plan: open or closed?
4. Decide on your launch style. Are you a Super Minimalist or a Super Whizz-Bang launcher? Maybe during different times of the year, that changes.
5. Which type of promotional tactics and strategies appeal most to you? Pick a few to try out during your first launch.

PART V

RETAIN YOUR PEOPLE

Now that you have all of these amazing people in your membership, the question becomes, how do you keep them happy and paying month after month? Recurring revenue only compounds if people stick around. This is where most people get sloppy, but it's actually where you want to stay sharp. So many business owners make the mistake of only focusing their attention and energy on getting members and not enough energy on keeping their existing members happy (and paying). That's a good way to get lots of sign-ups—and lots of cancellations.

Hopefully, you know by now that a lot of what we've discussed already contributes to retention. Your Success Map, getting people quick wins, content delivery, etc.—it all affects how people experience your membership and how happy they are with it. In Part V we're going to get even more specific and talk about tactics to keep people experiencing progress and interested in the next month's content. The focus boils down to two core goals: drive content consumption and community engagement. We'll get into strategies around community, content, communication, and pricing and how each of those can increase your retention. We'll also discuss the importance of onboarding—people's very first experience of your membership—which can dramatically impact their perspective (and therefore, lifetime value). And lastly, I'll tell you how to manage growth. Because you and I both know that you can grow this thing as big as you want—the sky's the limit.

Buckle up and come with me into the world of membership retention. And never forget, all we're doing here is continuing to help people have a good experience. That's the bottom line. Let's get into it.

CHAPTER 33

UNLOCKING MASSIVE PROFITS WITH A 1% RETENTION BOOST

If you're not convinced that retention is all that important to growing your membership, think about this: What if a mere 1 percent increase in retention could spell the difference between your membership just scraping by or skyrocketing to success? Well, I'm here to tell you, it can!

I've got to give a big shout-out to Scotty the Body, aka Scott Paley, for shining a bright light on this critical aspect of our membership world. He's been part of our community for years, and what makes this community so amazing is that we all learn and grow together. We share our collective knowledge, and Scott's wisdom about retention has been an absolute game-changer.

A while back, Scott gave a presentation about his membership. It started at $30 a month, had a thousand members, and was growing by a hundred members each month. But then Scott brought out the charts showing retention rates from 90 percent all the way up to 98 percent. The difference in the growth of the membership based on retention rate was mind-blowing. A 96 percent retention rate versus 99 percent? That could more than quadruple the number of members in your membership. Going up just a few percentage points in retention could triple the bottom line. That's the kind of math I like.

Now, you might be thinking, "Stu, how's that even possible? How could a 1 percent increase make such a massive difference?" Well, it's simple math, my friend. The first threshold we want to reach is 90 percent retention, but every single percent after that is a rocket booster for your membership.

At predictableprofitsbook.com, you're going to find a handy-dandy membership calculator that can help you visualize the impact of what we're talking about here. It takes into account things like your price and how many members you're starting with, how many you're adding and losing, and so much more.

But here's the bottom line: retention matters, and it's something you've got to be laser-focused on. This is the hidden gem, the golden ticket, whatever you want to call it—it's a must for your membership's success. In the upcoming chapters, we're going to get our hands dirty with some practical strategies that you can put into action to boost your retention.

So, here's your homework: check out the calculator and start crunching your own numbers. How much would your monthly revenue increase if you improved your retention rate by just 1 percent? Then, we'll get into some strategies to do just that.

CHAPTER 34

CONTENT RETENTION STRATEGIES

A whole bunch of years ago after I had just graduated university, I was looking to learn how to build my very first business, which was a speaking business. I used to travel around to high schools and colleges and deliver motivational talks.

Honestly, I didn't know anything about building a business. So I attended a seminar led by a gentleman by the name of John Childers, who was teaching how to grow a speaking business. And I was an absolute sponge. I soaked up everything that he was sharing. And then at the end of the event, he offered a membership that we could join. The membership solved an ongoing problem that so many of us had, which was the need for additional products we could include as part of a speaking package.

As part of this membership, John would provide us books on topics that virtually every speaker could use (things like success and time management). We would then have the recording rights to these books and could sell them as mini courses or include them in an upsell offer for anyone booking us to speak. It was a great idea that would instantly help us be able to charge a lot more per speaking engagement. I wanted in, and I had tons of ideas of how I could use this material to increase my offers. But it was a pretty expensive membership at about $300 a month. Now, you gotta remember, I had just graduated university. I barely had any money to my name, so $300 a month felt like a *big* commitment.

That's when I came up with a simple plan. I was going to join for the first month, and then I'd get one book and cancel. That'd be enough for me to gain one audio course to offer my customers. So I signed up for the membership, and I put it on my credit card, and sure enough, that first month he delivered the first book. But he also delivered a little "extra"—chapters 1 through 12 of a second book.

By delivering one-and-a-half books that first month, he overdelivered on his promise of one book. But guess what happened? I thought, *But now, I've only got half of the second book. Okay. I'll wait around for month two so I can get the second half of book number two.* But in that second month he delivered the second half of book two and also included the first half of the third book. It was genius and he had me hooked. I couldn't just have half a book!

I ended up staying in that membership month after month after month because psychologically, I had to close the loop. John put on a masterclass in getting your members to stick around by using his content to keep his members hooked. You can do the same through a variety of ways—and that's what we're going to dive into right now.

OVERLAPPING CONTENT

John's methodology with sending half a book month by month is an example of overlapping content. You can use the same principle with lessons or courses, where you overlap their release by months. So think about delivering a two-part training where Part 1 would be delivered in month one with Part 2 coming in month two. Make sense? This signals that the lesson is "incomplete" with just Part 1, and it keeps people wanting more because it opens a loop that rewards staying versus dipping out after the first few days.

FOCUS ON A QUICK WIN

Another powerful strategy is focusing on a quick win. We've touched on this plenty already. When somebody joins your community, what could you do to help them experience a quick win so that they've got that little bit of momentum on their side? The earlier people experience that win, the better! Inside The Membership Experience, you can feel the momentum that comes from somebody doing their founding member launch. It's an exhilarating, contagious feeling. In your own membership, what could you walk people through to help them get a quick win as early as possible? It might be completing a certain task, worksheet, or project, or it might be reaching a milestone. Keep it simple. And when they do get that win, don't forget to celebrate them!

RITUALISTIC CONTENT

Ritualistic content is delivered on a set schedule in the same way every time. If you have a podcast and stop publishing regularly, chances are, you'll hear from your listeners. That's what happened to me. I was on a regular rhythm of two podcast episodes a week. Then I took an unannounced break, and sure enough, I started getting messages from people. I had become part of their regular ritual each week while walking, driving, cleaning, etc. The same is true inside of your membership site. When you publish content on a regular schedule, it creates a rhythm for the membership as a whole. They begin to form daily consumption habits around your content—and that leads to a membership they don't want to leave.

MAKE YOUR CONTENT CONVENIENT

Different people like to learn in different ways, and it also increases the accessibility of your content in general. Account for that. Provide the text, audio, and video versions for all your content to give people options. And always have captions. According to a recent study, close to 92 percent of people report viewing videos on their phone with the sound off. If you are not accounting for that, then you're missing out on an important way to keep a huge portion of your audience engaged. **If people don't consume your content, it's hard for them to get any value. And if they don't get any value, they will leave.** Some people prefer to read. Others like to listen or watch. So make it easy for them to consume your content in the way they like.

MAKE YOUR CONTENT SEARCHABLE

If people can't find what they're looking for inside your membership, they'll get frustrated and will leave. That's a big reason why we built Membership.io with powerful search features. We want people to have access to a traditional search by title or description. But we also want them to be able to search inside video and audio as well. Meaning, if they remembered something you said and typed in a keyword, they would be brought to the moment in videos where you mentioned that exact word. That makes it easy for people to find the specific content they're looking for. When you can make it easy for people to consume your content, more people will consume it!

INVOLVE YOUR MEMBERS

Let your members help you with the creation of your content. That's one of the main benefits of the founding member launch! People are eager to get involved by providing feedback. We've done this multiple times when I offer a survey that asks people to contribute and share some of their best tactics and strategies throughout the year. For example, we've asked people to share their best retention strategies, or their best marketing or community strategies. Then we curate all that content and turn it into a guide. You can easily do the same. Tap into that collective wisdom and compile it into a resource for the whole membership.

SURPRISES AND DELIGHTS

Another thing that I encourage you to do is deliver different "surprises and delights" inside of your membership. These are unexpected bonuses, treats, or nuggets of value that your members are not expecting. For example, Russell Brunson sends his members a big ol' box of marketing books and goodies by mail. Other people in our community have provided timely bonuses at key intervals (often just after the renewal of month 1). We've also provided our members hidden "Easter eggs" within our content. Meaning, we'd hide extra surprises, and they'd discover them only if they watched certain content. By the way, the moment people discover these hidden surprises, it immediately creates a positive reaction. And many times they'll quickly go and tell someone!

These surprises can also be fun experiences. Take the "mundane" parts of your sign-up process and ask yourself, *How can we make this fun and memorable?* I encourage you to go to the online book resources at predictableprofitsbook.com, and you'll see some examples of our past thank-you videos. Instead of it being a boring "thanks for joining" video, we spend the extra effort to make the thank-you video fun and memorable. And these kinds of surprises get your members talking and gushing about you in the community (and often outside of the community as well).

Be intentional about it and try not to make them predictable. What can you offer that they won't expect? How can you overdeliver and impress them? What bonuses could you add that you don't even advertise, but where they just stumble upon them? This is so fun and a great way to show members some love.

TOOLS AND SOFTWARE

One of my very first customers in my first software company, AJ Brown, had a membership where he helped stock traders. A part of the trading process regularly took stock traders 20 minutes, and AJ had created a piece of software that cut it down to about 20 seconds. But the only way people could access that software was inside the membership. So many times, people joined just for that software. It served as a great retention point because people wouldn't leave due to the time they were saving from using this particular tool.

I recently joined another membership, and one of the big driving factors was access to a database that contained research on thousands of viral videos I could model for my own content. Sure, I could do the research myself. But this database saves me so much time—and it's continually updated.

So back to you . . . are there any tools or resources that you could create that are available only inside your members area? What process could you simplify with a tool or resource?

LIVE CONTENT

Live content gives you an opportunity to deepen the relationship you have with your members, but also the relationship your members have with each other. These could be live meetings or webinars on Zoom where your members are helping each other and engaging in conversations in smaller breakout rooms. Or this could be in-person meetups where your members are gathering with one another. Victoria Black and Gen Davidson did this in their membership SuperFastDiet. The women in their membership had been on this journey of losing weight together. So it was a super special experience to get together in person and connect. Bonny Snowdon did the same with her membership by gathering everyone for a one-day workshop where members worked on a particular art project. Heidi

Easley also does this with her annual member gala. Your members forge deeper relationships by creating these memories together.

How can you make your live content more of an experience—one that makes people want to keep showing up? Take inspiration from concerts and theater productions that you may have gone to, or live seminars and conferences. Think about all the different elements that are interwoven into these experiences. How can you make people look forward to showing up not only for what they're about to learn, but for the experience that they are about to have? And of course, as I've said before, you can always weave live experiences into impromptu meetups and gatherings.

As you can see, there are a whole bunch of things you can do with your content to boost retention. I want to encourage you to be creative and have fun with it. But don't forget, it's all about driving consumption of that content. The more content people consume, the more people are going to learn and the more progress they are going to make. Next up we're going to focus on communication strategies that will boost your overall retention.

GET THEM HOOKED

CHAPTER 35

COMMUNICATION RETENTION STRATEGIES

Communication is your best friend when it comes to keeping your members engaged and committed. It's the heartbeat of your membership, and it's how you maintain a thriving, close-knit community.

I want to start by debunking a common misconception about communication that came up when a client hired me to help grow their membership. They said, "Stu, I don't communicate with my members because when I do, it seems to remind them that they're part of the membership, and I see a surge in cancellations." Now, I was taken aback by this. How could communication possibly lead to cancellations? That's when I knew they really needed my help!

Turns out, the problem wasn't really the communication; it was something deeper. If your members are canceling their subscriptions because they're hearing from you, it's a sign of much bigger underlying issues. It suggests that they're not engaged with, don't see the value of, or haven't been using your membership. The last thing we want is for our members to forget they're part of our community. And we definitely don't want their first thought when they remember that they are to be, *I better cancel that.* **The key is to proactively keep your members engaged so that when they do hear from you, they're reminded of the value they receive, their journey, and how far they've come.**

Now let's dive into some communication strategies to help keep your members excited and committed.

STRATEGY 1: CONSISTENT WEEKLY COMMUNICATION

First and foremost, maintain a regular rhythm of communication with your members. I recommend a minimum of weekly communication. It's like tuning in to your favorite TV show on a specific day; it sets an expectation for your members. They anticipate your message and know you're actively engaged with them without bombarding their inboxes. In your weekly communication, here are some great things to do:

- *Share new content:* Keep your members informed about what's new inside the membership.
- *Highlight community discussions:* Showcase interesting or hot conversations happening in your community to encourage participation.
- *Celebrate wins:* Acknowledge and celebrate your members' achievements and milestones. Positive reinforcement goes a long way.

STRATEGY 2: TEASE UPCOMING CONTENT

Think about those binge-worthy Netflix series that you just can't stop watching. They often end with cliffhangers, leaving you eager to watch the next episode. You can create a similar feeling within your membership. Tease your upcoming content to create excitement and anticipation. This anticipation acts like a magnet, pulling your members to stay engaged and not miss out on what's next.

STRATEGY 3: PROMOTE LIVE EVENTS AND GATHERINGS

If you plan any in-person or live events, you must communicate about them with lots of enthusiasm. If you're not excited about them, why would you ever expect your members to get excited? These events are incredible opportunities to connect with your members on a deeper level and enhance their overall membership experience. Build anticipation and mystery around the event, and share the details early and often. Think of it as a launch with the goal of enticing your members to attend.

STRATEGY 4: STRATEGICALLY SCHEDULED AUTO RESPONDERS

As you grow your membership, you'll notice patterns where members often drop off at specific points. It's crucial to identify these drop-off points and preemptively intervene with strategically scheduled auto responders. So as your membership grows, start tracking the months that most people are dropping off. Was it immediately after month one? Or do you see members dropping off during month five? Once you identify your drop-off points, strategically have messages that get delivered right before they typically occur. The auto responders could include surprise bonuses, offers, or reminders of the value members receive. You could also speak to problems or challenges you know most members face at certain parts of their journey. These auto responders do the heavy lifting for you, rekindling your members' interest and keeping them moving forward.

STRATEGY 5: GET CREATIVE ABOUT FORMAT

A few unconventional communication methods can set you apart. Consider sending physical packages to your members. Physical mail is rare in this digital age, and when something tangible shows up, it has an impact. Whether it's a postcard, letter, or package with a little surprise (like stickers), it adds a personal touch and boosts the value of your membership.

Another powerful method is picking up the phone and calling your members. While this may not be feasible as your membership grows, it's a fantastic way to foster personal connections, especially in the early stages. Even as you scale, consider making calls to a select few members. And don't underestimate the impact of simple text messages or video and audio messages to brighten someone's day. We have time carved out of our schedule for either myself or someone on our team to send personalized messages to new members as well as members who might be at risk of canceling because they haven't logged into the membership for a while.

No matter the format, the goal is to build your relationship with them in a manner that will boost their awareness and engagement. Don't be afraid to talk to your members. They want to hear from you! So keep the conversation going with your customers, using effective communication as your ally.

CHAPTER 36

THE #1 PRICING STRATEGY FOR RETAINING MEMBERS

Now it's time to tackle one of the most powerful retention strategies of all: membership pricing.

Imagine you're starting your membership, and your founding member launch price is $20 a month. At this fantastic rate, you're great at attracting your early members. But what happens when, a week later, you decide to raise your prices to $25 a month? Well, these founding members can still enjoy their exclusive $20-a-month rate. And it gets better. As long as they remain members in good standing, they continue to pay $20 per month.

I started one of my memberships at $20 a month, then bumped the price to $25, eventually reaching $30, and finally, $47 a month. But those amazing folks who joined at the founding member price of $20 kept paying just that, even as the price for new members steadily rose. Can you imagine how they felt? They felt like they'd secured the deal of the century. And honestly, they did. The founding member launch price became a compelling retention strategy because people don't want to give up a good deal, especially one that keeps getting better over time.

Start low, and then gradually increase the price over time. Every time you raise the price, it's a reason to shout from the rooftops,

"Join before this date, and you'll be locked in at this low rate for as long as you remain a member in good standing." It becomes a powerful marketing strategy to bring people in, and it keeps your existing members motivated to stay.

One last tip: don't forget to remind your members about the fantastic deal they've secured. They are saving money every single month. Don't let them forget that. And if they do decide to cancel, remind them that they won't be able to rejoin at that price in the future. The feeling of having a deal that you don't want to lose is a retention strategy in itself.

In the grand scheme of retention strategies, pricing is the unsung hero that you should never overlook. Start low, raise your prices strategically, and reward early members who believed in your community. Your commitment to retaining your members will pay off, and every percentage point increase in retention can make a significant impact on your membership's profitability.

CHAPTER 37

COMMUNITY RETENTION STRATEGIES

The core of any community is to get people to consume your content and engage with each other. The better we do that, the stronger our retention game becomes. In this chapter, let's put on our tactical hats and explore the nitty-gritty tactics that will keep your members happy and sticking around like old friends.

Community Rituals: Just like I mentioned earlier with your content, you want to create rituals that keep your community members coming back for more. Regularly publish content at the same time; hold community meetups; establish a rhythm for your community that forms these habits. It can even be as simple as starting your videos with the same opening or experiences. For example, back in the day, the TV show *Cheers* always had that friendly song at the beginning of each episode (and if you've ever heard it, you're probably already singing it in your head, right?). That is an example of creating a ritual. In that show, everyone would also yell "Norm" whenever he entered the bar. That, too, is a ritual. In your membership, this could translate to you starting your online events with a fun poll or game, or having a weekly theme (e.g., Feedback Fridays or Sunday Spotlight), or perhaps celebrating a particular way after people reach certain milestones. Just make sure to do it consistently.

Insider Language: Inside jokes can became a huge, important, fun part of your membership culture that can create a bond. It's like having a secret handshake that only your members understand. You might have already noticed, but I say lots of quirky things on the regular like "just between us girls" or "hot diggitty dog" or "pitter patter, let's get at 'er." My community calls them Stu-isms. I had no idea I did this, but at a live event, a bunch of people stood up with Stu-isms written on their shirts! It was hilarious. These sayings have now become a part of our community language. It reinforces the feeling of being in a cool club we want to continue belonging to!

Community Identifiers: Think hats, T-shirts, mugs, sweatshirts, wristbands, or anything that members can use to show their pride in being part of your community. I'm pretty obsessed with my Peloton and have tons of Peloton gear. This works the same way. It's not only a symbol of belonging but can also raise money for charity if you donate the proceeds from the sale. That's what we do each year, and our community members love it. And here's a bonus tip: you could make "collector items" that are only available each year. That way members who've been in your membership for a while can show off their loyalty with pride!

Welcome Committees: Have you ever walked into a room and felt like the odd person out because you didn't know anybody? It's a little scary. This happened to me when my family moved from England to Canada when I started second grade. I was a terrified little kid walking into a new school in a new country. Then a kind boy named Matt came up and said hi. I told him I didn't know anyone and he said, "That's okay. I'll be your friend." I haven't forgotten it to this day, and Matt and I are still good friends. In fact, he was the best man in my wedding! Create a welcoming committee of your existing members who are eager to make newbies feel at home.

Participation Points and Leaderboards: Award points for various actions like consuming content, logging in, or finishing modules. Make it fun and engaging, and use leaderboards to create a little friendly competition among members. You could have badges people achieve, challenges, or contests—anything to create a sense of shared goals for members to rally around and connect with each other. You can manually track these things, but as your membership grows, I encourage you to explore a platform like Membership.io that has these features built right in and delivers the badges automatically after members take certain actions.

Accountability Partners and Groups: Facilitate accountability partnerships and groups within your community. It's a powerful way for members to help each other stay on track and build deeper relationships within the group.

Members Directory: Give your members visibility within the community by creating a member directory. They can search for other members near them, those with shared interests, or people at a similar stage in their journey. We even use our directory as a way to help facilitate networking for members interested in collaborating with one another.

Member Spotlights: Highlight different members regularly. This provides another means for members to get to know each other and have opportunities for connection. Sometimes we'll do this on our live calls, and other times we'll do this in our weekly communication to all members. It makes the spotlighted member feel appreciated and many times leads to connections with other members.

Share Wins: Designate a specific space where members can share their victories and celebrate one another's successes. Perhaps you could make it a weekly post or section of your forum or chat board? We'll also share wins on live calls to encourage and inspire people. Wins are great! We're all about wins! Find as many ways as you can to make a big deal of them.

Annual Awards Ceremony: Consider having an annual awards ceremony where you recognize and celebrate members' achievements. It's a great motivator and recognition tool and can be super fun. We create specific awards for certain achievements. An example would be our "Better Together" award, which is given to a member each month who has been going out of their way to help other members. And one of the most special awards is our Impact Award. It's given out once a year to the member who's had a huge impact in their community through a nonprofit or organization. The first year we gave it to a member named Kasey Hope. For every person who signed up for her membership, Kasey donated a meal to a child in Honduras. Talk about impact! You can do something similar and create meaningful awards for your community members.

But while each of these strategies is powerful, don't feel like you have to implement all of them at once. Cherry-pick the ones that resonate with you, and start with the simplest ones first. Retention is the sum of many parts, not just one strategy. Also, feel free to riff on each idea and create your own! These are meant to be jumping-off points. You can take each one as deep as you want.

PEOPLE COME FOR THE CONTENT AND STAY FOR THE COMMUNITY

CHAPTER 38

HOW TO TRIPLE THE LIFETIME VALUE OF A MEMBER IN THE FIRST 30 DAYS

In the first few moments when someone new joins a community, there's often a nervous energy and excitement. They may not know anyone, so it's your job to make them feel as welcome as possible right from the start by connecting and engaging them with other members and also by diving them into your content from the moment they join your membership.

The positive experience of joining a membership can come from a number of things like developing a connection with others, having an "aha" moment, or experiencing a small win, but right now we're going to focus on the connection factor. Here are only some of the *many* strategies that you could take.

Create a Thank-You Page Video. I mentioned this earlier, but I believe this video can have a profound impact on the way your members think about your membership. The essence of the video is to thank people for joining. But there is a bigger opportunity because this video begins to set the tone for your community. It's where you communicate the vibe and immerse people in your community's culture. Spend time making this video engaging and creative. Both show and tell people how you want them to engage with and experience your membership. What do you want them to think and feel? Use those thoughts and feelings to frame their experience. It's also a great opportunity to remind them all the benefits of your membership.

Establish Onboarding Steps and Activities. Create a clear onboarding path for your new members. Limit the number of options and choices to eliminate any confusion or doubt about what their next step should be. There are different ways and flows for onboarding, but it's all about one step clearly and logically leading to another, guiding members through the process in a way that is realistic and doable. What you don't want is to just give people access to the entire membership all at once without a proper orientation. That would instantly create overwhelm. You must keep the onboarding streamlined. For example, our 4-step onboarding process consists of: profile setup, password setup, onboarding survey, and welcome video. Somebody can't click anywhere but the next step. It ensures new members see what we want them to see during that onboarding flow.

Have a Welcome Celebration. I love this one and go all out for my welcome celebrations! We host a live party after cart close for our TME+ membership, and it's a total blast. I encourage you to do the same, especially if you have a closed marketing plan. Make it high-energy and set the stage for what members can expect and how to get the most out of their membership. You can bring in existing members to share their experiences and successes.

Visit predictableprofitsbook.com for examples from our community.

Use Bingo Cards. Creating a bingo card is a fun way to keep members engaged and working toward a sense of accomplishment with various activities they need to complete. These activities should include onboarding steps and participation in the discussion group. Consider what the perfect member would do inside of your community and put the most important and engaging things on the bingo card. You'll also want to give people some kind of reward for completing them.

Encourage Member Introductions. You definitely want people to introduce themselves when they join, but there is a nuance to making this more effective. Provide a framework for them to answer specific questions. These questions should focus on creating connection points, such as shared experiences or goals. Give each member the same list of questions to answer, like who they are, what they're interested in, and what brought them to this community. You can provide these as a first step when they join your discussion area.

Use Follow-Up E-mails. Send follow-up welcome e-mails to new members. These can include important information about the community, links to resources, and next steps. I also like to encourage new members early to "whitelist" the e-mail address used for member communications. We just don't want your e-mails going into the spam folder.

Deliver Awesome Customer Support. New customers will inevitably have questions. Clear communication channels for support issues are essential. Let members know how to contact customer support and make sure it gets them the help they need. My favorite way to support people is by leveraging our library of content. We use our software Membership.io to enable our members to ask any question at any time through a "wisdom chat." The software goes through our library of content, finds the information that's relevant to the question being asked (maybe a bit from a video, podcast, or recorded Q&A), then it stitches it together in a complete response. We even reference the videos, podcasts, and Q&As that inform the main answer that we're giving. This provides a far better experience for our members, but overnight, it also cut the amount of support requests we were getting into our help desk by over 90 percent! Bottom line, make it easy for people to find the answers they need.

CHAPTER 39

THE FIVE ESSENTIALS OF A THRIVING COMMUNITY

One of the best ways to keep your customers around and subscribed month after month is to create a community that people *actually* want to be part of. When I first began helping people grow their membership sites, I noticed the memberships with the highest retention rates were memberships that had highly engaged communities. That's when I realized that **people come for the content, but they stay for the community.** Thriving communities not only make the experience of your membership more fun for everyone, but they also lead to your members making a heck of a lot more progress toward their desired outcome.

Creating a vibrant, engaged, and supportive group of like-minded individuals doesn't happen by accident. Engaged communities are built on purpose and with intention. Here are five key elements that you should have in place.

1) CLEAR PURPOSE

Your community's purpose is to guide your members from where they are now, with their problems and challenges, all the way to where they want to be in the future, where those problems are solved and they've mastered new skills or arrived at their final destination. It's our North Star. But here's the thing—we can't just mention it once and call it a day. We have to communicate that purpose often. It's easy for people to get off track and forget, especially when they might feel like they're falling behind or struggling. Our job is to remind them that it's a journey, not a race, and that comparing themselves to others in the community is a distraction. We're all on our unique path, and it's our job to help them stay focused on that Success Path and recognize the progress that they are making. As my friend Gail Hyatt said, "People lose their way when they lose their why." Keep them focused on their "why."

> ***Our job is to remind them that it's a journey, not a race.***

2) A DEFINED CULTURE

Years ago, when we started our community, I was nervous and excited. And wouldn't you know it, by accident, I planned a family getaway right after the big launch. Words of advice: don't do that. Anyway, the community's excitement and engagement were through the roof, and I wanted to be involved, but my wife wanted me to relax and be present with our family (totally understandable). But between us, I couldn't help myself. Our community was buzzing with excitement from one of our most successful promotions ever, and we had welcomed thousands of people into our community. So there I was, sneaking peeks at my phone in the wee hours of the morning, trying not to get caught by my family before they woke up. But as I was scanning through, I saw a member who wasn't happy and felt compelled to tell everyone about it. I'm all for members sharing their thoughts, good and bad. And I think it's important for us to have a community where people from all backgrounds and experience levels feel safe to share and learn from each other. But the problem here was not so much what was being said, but how it was being said. In this case, it was rude, disrespectful, and even offensive.

Right away I knew this wasn't good and I needed to sort out the situation quickly. The member's extreme negativity and rudeness to others was impacting the experience of those who *were* excited to be there, and it was putting a major damper on the positive energy of everyone just entering the program. And based on how she responded to my team's efforts and responses, I could see that no matter what we did or didn't do, this person wasn't going to be happy. So I asked my team to issue her a full refund and remove her from the community immediately. Then I personally reached out to her and informed her of what we were doing. As you can imagine, she wasn't happy about that, either. But here's the thing: you have to protect the culture of your community. I want a community of people who are kind and respectful, and who are helping each other work toward a common goal or outcome.

Immediately after this happened, I realized this was also an opportunity. So without revealing any names or specifics about this particular situation, I taught a lesson to the whole community about how *not* to show up. Plus, I went into detail about how members could show up for themselves and each other, reinforcing our positive, respectful, and supportive culture.

We all have to be crystal clear about the culture we want to create. At my company, we want to encourage people to engage, step outside their comfort zones, and take action. We aim to create a culture of progress, where everyone is moving forward, implementing the next steps on their membership journey . . . and therefore achieving results. What kind of culture do you want in your community? It will only become a reality if you clearly communicate and provide the foundation for it.

3) CLEAR LEADERSHIP

Leading a community isn't always smooth sailing. Sometimes we have to have tough conversations and deal with conflicts. We need to step up and lead, even when it's uncomfortable. Generally, I'm a happy-go-lucky guy who prefers to avoid conflict, but I still make the effort to be transparent, say when we don't have all the answers, and engage in difficult conversations.

One of the toughest moments I've ever experienced growing a membership community involved discussions around the Black Lives Matter movement. People had very strong opinions, and any discussion that was brought up in the community was polarizing. You had people who believed strongly one way and others who felt the opposite. Our community manager Shana and I were up late multiple nights trying to figure out how we would navigate the situation.

Then it got very personal. My son Sam was born in South Africa. I'll just say some community members said very hurtful things. Inside, I was furious. Truthfully, I was ready to shut the whole membership down. But it's in these moments that people look to us for leadership. It's about holding space for these moments and addressing issues instead of sweeping them under the rug. That's why I held a live discussion for our community to come together and hear the perspectives of all sides. I was so scared. I had no idea how it would play out, but I knew that it was important to remain calm. I had to demonstrate to our whole community how to hold space for a discussion . . . even if I didn't agree with what someone was saying.

I also had help from Kimberly McCormick, a member of our community who has since become a wonderful friend and advisor. She helped mediate the two extreme opinions of the other guests, and it gave us an opportunity to demonstrate how we could have a discussion about some very hard things, but in a very respectable way. That's why I did it. It wasn't because I don't think tough conversations should happen or that people should think this way or that. I did it to demonstrate "how" to have tough conversations in a respectable way—even if you have polar opposite views. And it wasn't easy. Inside I was furious at what this one woman had said about my son and our family. But I had to remain calm, and it paid off in the long run. Our community came together in an incredible way. Step into your leadership role and demonstrate how you want your community to show up.

4) CLEAR RULES AND GUIDELINES

Clear rules and guidelines are crucial for a well-functioning community. They create a structure for engagement and help ensure everyone is on the same page regarding appropriate behavior. The great thing about this being *your* community is that *you* get to set the rules, so don't apologize for having them. Use them to help shape the kind of community you want to create. For example, we don't allow selling in our community because we don't want it to become a constant pitch fest. That wouldn't benefit our members at all or encourage connection and progress, especially if we had thousands of members doing it every single day. So when you're thinking about your rules and guidelines, ask yourself, *If everyone did XYZ, would it add to the experience or take away from the experience we're trying to create?* Think about your rules and communicate them clearly from the start.

5) CELEBRATION

Once your members are engaging and experiencing progress inside your thriving community, you'll want to capture and amplify it. This isn't just about making a bunch of money as a membership site owner; it's about making a real impact on people's lives. When your members can look back and see how far they've come, it's not just inspiring; it's a testament to what's possible in a remarkably short period of time. That's right, my friend, we're talking about stories again. These stories are a beacon for new members.

The bottom line is that when someone shares a story or win, capture it. Screenshot it, download it, save it, whatever. Just do it immediately or you'll forget. Create a dedicated folder each year to organize your growing collection of member success stories. As your community and stories grow, it might make sense to use more advanced tools, like Google Docs, spreadsheets, or databases. The goal is to keep track of these stories; they're the heartbeat of your community and business. The key is to develop a process where you capture these screenshots as they happen so that you can refer back to them. Because trust me when I say you'll forget if you don't. Having a set process makes the retrieval process *so* much easier.

Now, here's the fun part—use these stories to power your community and business. In your paid communities, celebrate the successes. Highlight them in monthly Q&A calls, showcase members who are making progress, and make feel-good moments. In your external marketing, share real stories in your ads (with permission). Let the world see that real people are getting real results from your community. Close that Circle of Awesomeness.

On a more personal level, these community stories aren't just for others; they can be a source of strength and a good reminder for you too. There are plenty of moments in the journey of building a membership when things don't go as planned. When I'm feeling down, I turn to our Slack channel where we store our members' success stories. I read them and think about the incredible transformations our community has witnessed.

When you connect with the transformations you're helping make possible, it can really be moving. It's a powerful reminder of why we do what we do and renews our focus on helping our members achieve their goals. These stories will be your fuel if you start to doubt yourself and your mission. In those tough moments, the best way to snap out of it is to revisit your members' success stories.

All right, now that you have established a strong community, how do you get to them to actually *engage*? We'll cover that in the next chapter.

CHAPTER 40

WINNING STRATEGIES TO BOOST COMMUNITY ENGAGEMENT

Now that you've effectively created connection within your community, let's get into how to spark their engagement and get people talking. Hopefully, your engagement takes off naturally, and your community is already rocking and rolling. But what happens when it's not? Or what happens when the energy fizzles, and there's not the kind of engagement that you're looking for? Or what if it doesn't even ignite from the beginning? It's essential to recognize that all of these scenarios can happen, and it's okay. Even when your community's energy is high, it's important to strategically support and encourage community engagement. Here are some key strategies to get things moving.

YOU MUST GO FIRST

In any community, you, as the community leader, must be the one to go first. You need to demonstrate the kind of culture and engagement you want to create. Especially in the beginning, you'll need to be more vulnerable, share more about yourself, and take the initiative in sparking discussions. The "lurkers" are often waiting for someone else to go first. That must be you. Over time, your momentum will inspire your community to do the same.

A perfect example of this was when I shared with our community some of the struggles that I personally had during the COVID restrictions. For the first time in my life, I went into a serious funk. I would walk the kids to school every morning, ride my Peloton for an hour, and then literally sit in the same chair and stare out the window for the rest of the day. It was the strangest thing. To make matters worse, I knew I was struggling but felt embarrassed and hadn't shared it before with anyone, not even Amy. It took a few months, but eventually I started to get back to myself. And a few months after that, I decided I would share what I experienced with my community. The support was incredible. But the best part was the fact that it set the stage for others to share on a deeper level as well.

If you're wanting your community to open up but you're closed off, it doesn't really model the kind of actions you want see. However, if you go first, it serves as an open invitation for your members to do the same.

REIGNITING THE CULTURE

If your community has been around for some time and you see a drop in engagement, it's time to reignite the culture. Embrace the unique aspects of your community and bring them to the forefront. Use fun sayings, inside jokes, or any shared cultural elements to reconnect members.

For one of our memberships, we could feel things were getting a little stale and attendance started to drop for our live elements like our Q&A sessions. So we went back to the drawing board and reimagined our live deliverables. It also gave us a chance to infuse our culture and values into our content, and particularly the value of fun. The result was turning our monthly Q&A where I would answer questions for 90 minutes into a quarterly one-day event. This created space for us to get more creative with what we delivered. We added funny commercials for our programs, content "performed" by the team, hilarious updates, live interactive polls, quizzes, giveaways, and so much more. It was a resounding success. Our community *loved* it, and we could immediately feel the energy and culture was back.

SHOW YOU CARE

Showing behind-the-scenes glimpses expresses how much you care about the community's experience and helps them understand the "why" behind your efforts. This is especially important when you make changes to the membership. You want your members to know why you're making the changes and why it's in their best interests. Never be afraid of making changes, because you're only making the changes to improve the experience. And when you explain why you're making those changes, it demonstrates that there is some actual thought behind it. It demonstrates that you care.

RECONNECTING TO THE OUTCOME

Members join your community with the goal of achieving a particular outcome. It's common for them to lose touch with that goal over time. Challenge them to reconnect with their "why" by organizing events like challenges, hot seats, accountability groups, or discussion sessions. As we've discussed several times, creating a culture of progress is essential. Measure and reward members for reaching milestones or goals, and encourage them to share their progress with the community.

I find many people struggle to share their wins. They don't want to be perceived as bragging. So one of the best ways you can show you care is to celebrate people so they don't have to initiate it themselves. You want them to know that it's not bragging, but instead it's inspiring others and showing them what's possible. Make your community a safe place for members to celebrate their successes and keep them connected to the outcome they're after.

LIVE EVENTS AND MEETUPS

Live events can be a game-changer for community engagement. Organize big live events or simple local meetups. These gatherings give members a chance to connect in person and share their experiences. Facilitating local meetups for members in the same area will strengthen local connections. Carrie Green does a beautiful job of this in her membership called Female Entrepreneurs Association. She facilitates local meetups and gatherings so that people from various cities and countries can get together (without Carrie actually being there herself). And you can do the same as well. It's one of the reasons I recommend having a members' directory. We use the one built right into Membership.io, which gives members the ability to connect with one another in a variety of ways, including being able to find members who might live nearby (they can choose to share their city or not). We also proactively hold meetups—one year in London, England, we had over 100 members come out and connect. Nothing will deepen connection faster than meeting in person, so look for opportunities where you can facilitate this.

SCAVENGER HUNTS AND SOCIAL POSTS

Periodically, we use scavenger hunts or bingo cards to reignite engagement. Lisa Breitenfeldt regularly does this with her geocaching membership. This market was new to me until I met Lisa, but essentially, it's like a real-life scavenger hunt. Imagine people following a variety of clues and discovering hidden treasures.

Similarly, you can encourage members to share personal stories, photos, or opinions that create interaction and discussion, particularly centered around common interests. A simple example of this was when we shared a post of me carrying the kids on a "double-decker piggyback." The caption read, "Who else is going into the weekend to have some fun with your kids? Share your pics below."

REACH OUT TO DISENGAGED MEMBERS

Sometimes members who were previously highly engaged start to disengage. Reach out to them with a simple message asking if everything is okay. A small gesture like this can reignite their involvement in the community. We also do this with short video or audio messages. This is why it's important to track the activity of your members because then you'll have insights into which members are at risk for potentially canceling because they're not engaged.

As always, you don't have to do all of these methods at once. Use the strategies that resonate with you and your community, and be open to adjusting your process as you learn and grow as a membership site owner. The key is to create a positive, engaging experience from the very beginning to help your members connect and engage effectively. You can do this by keeping the fun alive and encouraging your community members to share their stories.

CHAPTER 41

MANAGING GROWTH

I can honestly say I've been there, from the early days with just a handful of members to a bustling community with thousands of folks eager to connect and share their passions. One day, you'll be there too. Maybe you already are. While having thousands of members is *awesome*, managing that growth is tricky and can feel overwhelming. I'm here to equip you with some super simple strategies that will help you master this ever-changing landscape, and the easiest way to approach this is to think of your community growth in phases.

PHASE ONE: YOU'RE THE CAPTAIN

It starts with you, my friend. At the start of your membership, you're the one-person show managing that community. In these early days, one of the most critical things to remember is to set the right expectations. Now, I understand you're eager to help and provide support 24/7. But we've all got lives outside our online world, right? Creating the expectation that you'll be at your community's beck and call around the clock can be a double-edged sword. It's not just about maintaining your sanity but also the health and growth of your community. When you become the go-to for every little query, your members might not engage with each other.

In the early days, my community had this unspoken rule that my team was available, even on weekends. But then I decided to set things straight.

I went into the community and laid it out honestly. I explained that our businesses are designed to give us time with our loved ones, and that means taking weekends off. Some posts might remain unanswered until the start of the week. But this was as much for our benefit as it was for theirs. And you know what happened? Our community rallied behind the decision, thanking us for protecting that precious family time. So my advice to you is simple—establish your boundaries early. For us, weekends are sacred family time, and we make that clear. However you want your community to run, do it that way from day one.

Lastly, remember to leverage tools that also give you time back. For example, we use Membership.io's Wisdom feature to handle all incoming questions from the community. And most of the time, our community members find exactly what they need without needing any additional support from me or my team.

PHASE TWO: BUILD YOUR VOLUNTEER TEAM

You might find that as your community grows, you can't do it all on your own. That's where Phase Two comes in: the volunteer team. You've got those incredible individuals, your power users, who bring your community to life. They're engaged, responsive, and just fabulous. If you're feeling like you need some help but aren't quite sure it's time to hire yet, it's time to gather and mobilize them.

One brilliant thing we did in our community was create what we call our Ambassador Team. These are the folks who've gone through our Membership Experience, so they know the ropes. They offer a personal touch to the community that's hard to maintain if you're a one-person show. They welcome new members, create a warm atmosphere, and guide the members through their journey.

Your Ambassador Team will be your unsung heroes, and you have to make sure you show them love and appreciation. After all, they're investing time and effort to make your community vibrant. Small notes of appreciation, little gifts, regular communication—all of these are ways to take care of your ambassadors. You can also distinguish them in your community with special badges. Remember, they're not in it for the perks, but it's your job to make them feel special. The perks and their unique role can motivate them to be your community's guiding lights.

Empower your Ambassador Team with the tools and information they need to represent you effectively. Create an FAQ document, complete with common questions and responses. This equips them to step in and help, just like you would.

PHASE THREE: WELCOME YOUR COMMUNITY MANAGER

There will come a point where you need a dedicated team member to run your community—a Community Manager. But let me share a piece of advice I got from a mentor of mine. He said, "Don't go into it, grow into it." Make sure that you've first laid a solid foundation, built processes, and documented best practices. A Community Manager's role is to oversee your Ambassador Team, boost engagement, and elevate the community's experience.

Your Community Manager is more than just a team member. They are a prominent figure in your community, so introduce them properly. Ensure that your community knows who they are and transfer your credibility to them. Let your community know that this person is as invested in their success as you are.

Hiring a Community Manager should be a gradual process. Start with a part-time role, and as your community's needs grow, you can evolve it into a full-time commitment. The processes you've already established will make onboarding your Community Manager smoother.

Managing your community is a journey, just like life. Your community—your baby!—will grow and evolve and become an ever-thriving ecosystem. With dedication, perseverance, and using the strategies now in your tool kit, your community will be able to grow smoothly. It's a key part in keeping your members around for years to come.

As we wrap up this retention section and you've navigated through a wealth of strategies, my final piece of advice is to reference predictableprofitsbook.com. These valuable road maps will help you choose the retention tactics that resonate with you and that you can easily implement in your membership.

Your journey doesn't end here. You're here because you care, not just about your business's profitability, but also about your community, your members, and their experiences. This is a continuous journey full of excitement and profitability, but also meaning and purpose.

ACTION STEPS

1. Check out the book resources on predictableprofitsbook.com and do a little membership math on what increasing your retention would do for your business.
2. Pick one content-retention strategy to implement.
3. Pick one communication-retention strategy to implement.
4. Pick one community-retention strategy to implement.
5. Raise your price and tell everyone to join before it goes up.
6. Create a welcome sequence.
7. Outline your community's purpose, culture, and rules and guidelines.
8. Understand what phase of growth you are in. Do you need to build a volunteer team or hire a community manager?

"DON'T GO INTO IT, GROW INTO IT"

—John Childers

CONCLUSION

Maximizing Your Impact

Helping you launch a successful membership site was the primary reason I wrote this book. (Duh, right?) Watching our clients and customers go from having just an idea to having a full-blown membership and building six-, seven-, and even eight-figure memberships has been truly inspiring. So much can happen in such a short period of time if you put what you've learned from this book into practice.

But there is a second reason I wrote this book. I truly believe that the people who can have the biggest impact on this world are you and me—entrepreneurs who help people with our products. But there's another reason, and that is our unlimited earning potential. And that means our unlimited potential to give. That's what gets me fired up—using our skills to grow the membership and then using the money to impact the lives of those we care about most. That might mean creating incredible memories with your family, caring for elderly parents, or giving a close friend an experience of a lifetime. Whatever it is, a membership can help you get there.

Beyond that, a membership can also help you extend the ripple of your impact even further to causes and organizations that align with your values and are doing great work to make this world a better place. When you get to a place where you have predictable profits and are off the hamster wheel of one-time payments, you will have the ability to give even more to causes and people that you love and be a force for good. In my mind, being generous is the greatest benefit of all. **There are no limits on how much we can make—and therefore no limits on how much we can give!**

Years ago, when I was running my consulting business, I could not break a certain income level that I kept bumping up against. It was about $400,000 a year. Every time I got to that threshold, subconsciously my brain would say, "Whoa, Stuey, this is too much money. You're making too much money." At the time, I was still living in my parents' basement (don't judge, we all start somewhere!). Here's the awkward part of that story: at the time, that business was earning roughly twice as much as both my parents made combined. I had come from a blue-collar family, and nobody worked harder than my parents. There was a feeling of guilt that I was still living in their basement, making more than them, and not working anywhere near as hard. It was a subconscious block.

Deep down I felt like I didn't deserve it. Whenever I approached that $400,000 mark, I would unconsciously start doing silly things that would sabotage my success. I'd stop calling clients back or stop running marketing campaigns that I knew would work, and so my income would come right back down to $200,000 or so a year. That may or may not sound like a huge amount of money to you, but for me, my mind couldn't even fathom earning anything beyond $400,000, let alone building a million-dollar business.

Maybe you can relate to having a money block of some kind. If you've ever found yourself stuck at a certain income level and having a hard time breaking through, there might be something very powerful holding you back under the surface. It doesn't matter what your "number" is. It will change over time as you reach new heights. However, you've got to make some mental shifts; otherwise, you'll forever remain stuck. As my friend Bari Baumgardner says, "New level, new devil." You have to face your limiting beliefs and mental blocks at each new level you reach. If you can't get right with the purpose of money, then it doesn't matter how much money you want to make—you'll never get there because subconsciously, you'll sabotage yourself.

This cycle kept repeating itself, and I could never bust through until the very first time that Amy took me to Kenya. She has always traveled to remote areas of the world and had a passion to help bring educational opportunities to people in underserved communities. She used to be a teacher and is moved by the thousands of kids who want to go to school but just can't because the school's either too far or the parents need the kids to work to earn some money to survive.

When we traveled down there for the first time years ago, we partnered with a local woman named Irene to build a school. She's now been our partner with our charity for over 15 years. We call her the Mother Teresa of Africa. While touring the area one day, I found myself chatting with the chairman of one particular community. I said, "Out of curiosity, what does it cost to fund the full-time salary of a teacher?"

He thought about it for a moment and said, "About a hundred dollars a month."

"You mean for a hundred dollars a month, I could pay the full-time salary of a teacher who would then be able to educate a classroom of kids?"

"Yup," he said.

My mind went wild with possibility. At the time, my first software company was selling a single site license for $97. I thought, *Oh my gosh, if we just sell one more license of the software and I allocate that to funding the full-time salary of the teacher, imagine the impact that we could have.* That's when the light bulb really went off: *What if we make a whole lot more money? We'd have so much more to give!*

It was a huge turning point, because in that moment I realized that the more money I make, the more impact I can have. Almost in an instant, the guilt of making money was released. From that point forward, my business went from $400,000 being our max to the very next year generating millions of dollars in revenue.

MAKE YOUR BUSINESS A FORCE FOR GOOD

So how can you use your business as a force for good? From my experience, there are four main ways to make an impact.

1) With Your Money

The first way way you can make an impact is to write a check. Easy, right? This is what most people do. They personally give to causes they care about or give a percentage of their business's revenue to them. A dear friend and member of my high-level mastermind is a woman named Bonnie Christine. There are many amazing things about Bonnie, but the one I want to highlight here is that every year she gives away 10 percent of her gross revenue. A lot of people plan to do this. But then that money hits their bank account and it becomes harder and harder to give it away. And often, even as the business grows, they may give more from a dollar perspective, but the percentage goes down. They start to think, *Maybe I'll just give 9 percent or 8 percent and go get a new car.* Not Bonnie. As her business has grown to produce millions in revenue, the percentage she gives has stayed steady. Yes, that means she gives hundreds of thousands of dollars every year to people and causes she is passionate about. It's so inspiring.

2) With Your Team

The second way you can create impact is to involve your team. In our company, every quarter, whoever wants to present on behalf of a charity can throw their name in a hat. We then pick three people at random to deliver a quick five-minute presentation on behalf of the charity or cause that they're passionate about. The whole team then votes on who gets a donation. We allocate $10,000 for first place, and $2,500 for second and third place. Our team members then get to take that check to that cause they're passionate about. And through that, you're also going to discover the things that are important to your team. We've cut checks to a women's safe house, suicide prevention, ocean cleanup, pet shelters, and so many more. It's such an honor and an incredible bonding experience for our team too.

3) With Your Community

The third way is to involve your community. This is really powerful because as your community grows, so does your ability to be able to raise money together. We've done this in two different ways. The first is with an online fundraiser. We did a teleseminar where I brought six or seven of my friends together and shared their predictions for the next year. (This was even before Zoom!) People paid to have access, and all the money that we made just went straight to the cause. That first time around, I think we raised $14,000. This bought a school all new printers and computers and a fresh paint job, and covered the fees for 59 girls to attend. Now we do our prediction call every year, and we've raised over $400,000 from a single event!

The second way to involve your community is with live events. This is the primary way we fundraise for our charity. I often speak at events for my friends like Jeff Walker, Dean Graziosi, Russell Brunson, Michael Hyatt, and Amy Porterfield, and make an offer for something that the audience would want anyway, with all the proceeds going to charity. We've done split tests where we just ask people to straight donate or offer them a product where we donate the proceeds, and we always make more with an offer. If there's a thousand people in the room and do a straight ask for donations, we'll raise $30,000 or $40,000 if we're lucky. If we make an offer, we'll raise anywhere between $150,000 to $250,000.

4) With Your Business

The final way to create lasting impact with your money is with your business. This is where you weave a giving model directly into your business. There are tons of examples of this. Russell Brunson and Todd Dickerson from ClickFunnels are a perfect example, as they donate $1 for every funnel that goes live on their platform. They've done that since day one—and they've now donated millions of dollars. It's an incredibly generous way to raise money, because it's built right into the business model.

Kasey Hope has also done this with her membership. For every new member that joins, she donates a meal to an organization that serves kids experiencing food insecurity. Christie Hawkins does something similar with donating art supplies to underprivileged communities in Honduras. Ali Kay donates all the sales on the last day of her big launches to a charity she loves in Haiti (where her son was adopted from).

In our business, we do this by donating the first month of every member's subscription to Village Impact. We weave it right into the actual business so a portion of the revenue from every new customer goes to the charity. That's a great way to start if you're looking to implement this in your own business. Donate the first month to a cause you're passionate about and let your members know. Not because you're showing off or using it for smarmy marketing, but because you're proud and want to get all the money you can for this cause you believe in! People love to be a part of something good. Let them know where their money is going and that they're helping to make an impact.

There are all kinds of creative ways to make an impact with your money. Have you ever been to a pet store, and while you're checking out, they ask if you want to add $2 to help unhoused pets? It's like a top off for charity. You can get creative with this. The point that I hope you come away with is that a membership gives us plenty of ways to extend the impact we can have in this world. Start small, but definitely start. Can you imagine the impact that could be made if big-hearted entrepreneurs like you are out there using the money they make to give to people and organizations in need? It would create a ripple effect of epic proportions.

That's my greatest hope for you. That you not only create a membership that changes your life, but that in turn you generously give and change the world. Let's do it together, my friend.

USE YOUR BUSINESS FOR GOOD

RESOURCES

For additional resources like case studies, interviews, and tools to help you build your business, please visit
www.predictableprofitsbook.com

ENDNOTES

1. "The Subscription Economy Index," Subscribed Institute, March 2021, https://www.amic.media/media/files/file_352_2844.pdf.

2. Frankie Karrer, "98% of U.S. Consumers Subscribe to at Least One Streaming Service," *MNTN*, https://mountain.com/blog/98-of-u-s-consumers-subscribe-to-at-least-one-streaming-service/.

3. Daniela Coppola, "Number of Amazon Prime users in the United States from 2017 to 2022 with a forecast for 2023 and 2024 (in millions)," *Statista*, July 11, 2023, https://www.statista.com/statistics/504687/number-of-amazon-prime-subscription-households-usa/.

4. Luisa Zhou, "Small Business Statistics: The Ultimate List in 2024," *Luisa Zhou Blog*, updated March 25, 2024, https://luisazhou.com/blog/small-business-statistics/.

ACKNOWLEDGMENTS

An interesting thing happens when you write a book—you realize just how many people have helped or had an influence on your journey. For me that starts at home.

I'd first like to thank my amazing wife, Amy. Who knew that our conversation on a bus ride to Florida would lead to the life we've created together. Thank you for believing in me, encouraging me, and inspiring me to be the best version of myself. You've opened my eyes to the true impact we can have as entrepreneurs, and I'm so grateful for the way we love and grow together.

Next are my kids, Marla and Sam. My heart filled with joy when you entered my life, and I'm so stinking proud of the kind, determined, and hard-working individuals you're becoming. Don't ever stop dreaming and striving for the things you want to achieve. And thank you for our daily walks to school . . . I cherish that time together.

To Mum and Dad—a massive thank you. I was fortunate because I hit the "parent jackpot." Parents who worked so hard every day and yet never missed a soccer game, school event, or special moment. You've always encouraged me to be myself and gave me the confidence to chase my dreams. I love you.

Thanks, Faye, for always being such a loving sister who always brings the joy. I love our "friendly" games . . . but I love the giggles and laughs that come with them more.

To my in-laws Lynn and Dave, Nick and Ravindri, as well as my brother- and sister-in-law, Lynne and Jack, thank you for your love and support.

I would also like to thank Sheila Piesta who has single-handedly removed 90% of our household stress and created the space for us to pursue our big ideas. You're such an important part of our success.

Being in business for 20-plus years, I've been fortunate to have built some incredible friendships that have lasted the test of time. Amy Porterfield, Russell Brunson, Jeff Walker, Victoria Labalme, Dean Graziosi, Bonnie Christine, Ryan Levesque, Shaa Wasmund, Dan Martell, Michael Hyatt, and Megan Hyatt, thank you. Whether we were brainstorming in the Masai Mara, partnering on projects, raising money for charity, or strategizing for our next launch, our friendship means the world. You've each had a profound impact on me.

To my team. It's you who have brought these ideas to life. I feel so lucky to have a supportive team who cares so deeply about the work we get to do. My heart swells when I see your excitement for the success of our customers and clients. And it's always a plus when we get to share late-night giggles during a launch or the grind of climbing another mountain during 29029!

A special shout out to my two business partners, Andrew Ferraccioli and Asim Gilani. I love your brains, your grit, and most importantly, your heart. It's a blessing to have partners who care deeply about building a business that serves and gives at the highest levels. It still humbles me to think about how you've supported our charity, Village Impact, by covering the annual operating expenses every year. We've created an amazing business together, but I'm more excited about where it's all going. I appreciate you both more than you realize.

To my executive assistant, Summer, I owe you a lifetime of hugs for being my second brain, brainstorming partner, and calendar bodyguard. You ooze positivity and truly are a gift. I'm forever grateful for the way you keep me organized and on track.

On this journey I've had some incredible mentors and people who had a tremendous influence on me. Sometimes it was a single encounter and other times it developed into a lifelong friendship.

Big thank you to Bob Urichuck, Juri Chabursky, Vern Martin, John Childers, Armand Morin, Alex Mandossian, and John Reese.

However, there is one special mentor I'd like to single out—and that's Reid Tracy. I celebrate "Reid Day" every August 29th because of an e-mail offering a crazy-generous donation to our charity in exchange for teaching you and your team everything I knew about membership sites. That single gesture fundamentally changed my life. Words can't describe the impact you've had with your texts of encouragement, support for our charity, and business insights. My hope is to do you proud with this book and to continue the ripple effect of positivity.

Along with mentors, I've been fortunate to be part of many masterminds. My Plat mastermind is one that has been a lifeline for over 10 years. I cherish the relationships that have come from that group, and I'm so grateful for the collective wisdom that has been shared. Special shout-out to Bari Baumgardner, Blue Melnick, Michelle Falzon, Carrie Green, Ellyn Bader, Jason Friedman, John Gallagher, Susan Garrett, Annie Hyman Pratt, Brian Kurtz, Michael Maidens, Rick McFarland, Olivier Roland, Ricardo Teixeria, Farukh Shroff, Shelley Brander, Ruth Buczynski, Elliott Connie, Victor Damasio, Sebastien Night, Rachel Miller, Sigrun, Will Hamilton, Ocean Robbins, and so many others.

I'd also like to acknowledge my former business partner Tracy Childers. WishList Member gave me the foundation for what I get to do today. Thank you.

To the Hay House team, thank you so much. This book required a lot of patience, and I'm so grateful for your ability to guide this newbie author through the publishing process. And of course a special shout-out to Lisa Cheng and Monica O'Connor for helping me get it across the finish line.

To my writing partner, Liz Morrow, you are a gem. You're the consummate professional who made the writing of the book so easy and fun. One minute we're talking about membership strategy, then stories from within our community, and then we're wiping tears from our face because we're laughing so hard thanks to some cheesy joke. You've become a great friend, and I can't wait for the many books to come.

Lastly, I want to thank our incredible community. Your stories and the work that you're doing to help people in your memberships are what light me up. The collective ripple effect is massive, and little by little, we're making this world a better place.

Special shout-out to everyone in my IMPACT mastermind (many of whom are featured throughout this book): Alex Cattoni, Ali Kay, Ali Aungst, Dr. Ben Hardy, Beth Paynter-Magnetti, Bonnie Christine, Bonny Snowdon, Caitlin Mitchell, Danielle LaPorte, Debbie Steinberg Kuntz, Katrina Sequenzia, Leslie Vernick, Manuela-Victoire Fermely, Mark Groves, Megan Hyatt Miller, Nicholas Wilton, Peter Johnson, Ray Edwards, Sarah Williams, Scott Paley, Sharon Pope, Susan Bradley, and Suzi Dafnis. You are playing at the highest level and I love how you show up for each other.

Also, big high five to everyone in our Connect mastermind. It's inspiring watching you take an idea, apply it, and report back to the next meeting with eye-popping results. It's an honor to be on this journey with you, and one of my favorite things is our mastermind meetings.

To our extended TME community, thank you for giving me the opportunity to share. Keep moving forward, my friends. The work you're doing matters.

And lastly, I want to take a moment and thank you! You picked up this book for a reason. My guess is that you have something to share that could help others. Take what you've learned from this book and start your membership today. Remember, in the beginning, it's just an experiment. Don't overthink it. Keep it simple. Because just like when Reid Tracy believed in me before I believed in myself, I want you to know that you can 100% do this. Having recurring revenue can become your reality too, but you've got to get started. Wishing you all the best.

ABOUT THE AUTHOR

Stu McLaren is a membership expert and the co-founder of Membership.io, a leading platform serving thousands of online membership sites. With over 15 years of experience in the subscription industry, Stu coaches and consults best-selling authors, top-rated speakers, experts, hobbyists, and entrepreneurs on how to turn their expertise into predictable, recurring revenue. Stu lives just outside of Toronto, Canada, with his wife and two kids. Learn more at **Stu.me**.

Hay House Titles of Related Interest

THE SHIFT, the movie,
starring Dr. Wayne W. Dyer
(available as an online streaming video)
www.hayhouse.com/the-shift-movie

***

HIGH PERFORMANCE HABITS: How Extraordinary People Become That Way, by Brendon Burchard

DOTCOM SECRETS: Underground Playbook for Growing Your Company Online with Sales Funnels, by Russell Brunson

LAUNCH (UPDATED & EXPANDED EDITION): How to Sell Almost Anything Online, Build a Business You Love, and Live the Life of Your DreamS, by Jeff Walker

ONE BOX AT A TIME: How to Build and Grow a Thriving Subscription Box Business, by Sarah Williams

TWO WEEKS NOTICE: Find the Courage to Quit Your Job, Make More Money, Work Where You Want, and Change the World, by Amy Porterfield

All of the above are available at your local bookstore or may be ordered by visiting:

Hay House India: www.hayhouse.co.in
Hay House USA: www.hayhouse.com®
Hay House Australia: www.hayhouse.com.au
Hay House UK: www.hayhouse.co.uk

***

We hope you enjoyed this Hay House book. If you'd like to receive our online catalog featuring additional information on Hay House books and products, or if you'd like to find out more about the Hay Foundation, please contact:

Hay House Publishers (India) Pvt Ltd
Muskaan Complex, Plot No. 3,
B-2, Vasant Kunj, New Delhi 110 070
Phone: +91 11 41761620
www.hayhouse.co.in

—

Published in the United States by:
Hay House LLC, P.O. Box 5100, Carlsbad, CA 92018-5100
(760) 31-7695 or (800) 654-5126
www.hayhouse.com® • www.hayfoundation.org

Published in Australia by:
Hay House Australia Publishing Pty Ltd
18/36 Ralph St., Alexandria NSW 2015
Phone: +61 (02) 9669 4299
www.hayhouse.com.au

Published in the United Kingdom by:
Hay House UK Ltd
1st Floor, Crawford Corner,
91–93 Baker Street, London W1U 6QQ
Phone: +44 (0)20 3927 7290
www.hayhouse.co.uk

—